educate.ie

Parade
Christmas Annual 2024

Editor: Elaine Collins
Design and Layout: Karyn Moynihan
Cover Design: Kieran O'Donoghue
Stories, Poems and Feature Articles: © Elaine Collins
ISBN: 978-1-916832-74-9

© 2024 Educate.ie
Printed in Ireland by Walsh Colour Print, Castleisland, Co. Kerry
Freephone 1800 613 111

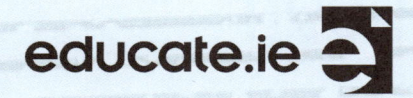

educate.ie

Artwork and Photos: Akis Melachris p18-19, 28; shutterstock.com

Without limiting the rights under copyright, this book is sold subject to the condition that it shall not, by way of trade or otherwise, be reproduced, stored in or introduced into a retrieval system, or transmitted, in any form or by any means (electronic, mechanical, photocopying, recording or otherwise), or otherwise circulated, without the publisher's prior consent, in any form other than that in which it is published and without a similar condition, including this condition, being imposed on the subsequent publisher.

The author and publisher have made every effort to trace all copyright owners, but if any material has inadvertently been reproduced without permission, they would be happy to make the necessary arrangement at the earliest opportunity, and encourage owners of copyright material not acknowledged to make contact.

The publisher does not provide warranty, express or implied, over the content of recipes and crafts in this publication. It is the responsibility of the reader and/or their parent/guardian to determine the value and quality of any recipe or craft instructions provided and to determine the nutritional value, if any, and safety of the preparation instructions.

The recipes and crafts presented are intended for entertainment and/or informational purposes and for use by persons having appropriate technical skill, at their own discretion and risk.

This Christmas annual belongs to ...

Name/Ainm/Imię/Ім'я:
_____

Age/Aois/Wiek/Вік: _____

School/Scoil/Szkoła/ Школа:
_____

I am in _____ Class.

Contents

Get ready for Christmas! 4
That's funny! 6
Santa Science 8
Make it! 10
Guess who? 12
Science & Nature Quiz 14
Puzail 15
Little Puds.............................16
The Jaguar Man........................18
Design 20
Dathaigh 21
Monster Maths 22
Tangled!................................23
Sports & Hobbies Quiz 24
Crosfhocal 25
Look again! 26
A Smash Hit!........................... 28
Dathaigh 30
Puzail 31
Aimsigh na Difríochtaí 32
How many?/Cé mhéad? 34
Winter Quiz............................35
That's funny! 36
Chocolate Chipping! 38
Puzail/Puzzles.........................40

Féach Arís!.............................42
What a load of nonsense! 44
Puzzles 46
Make it! 48
Snow Business 50
Snow poems...........................52
Souped up! 54
General Knowledge Quiz...............56
Tangled! 57
Féach Arís! 58
Something for everyone! 60
That's funny! 62
What's missing? 64
Cad atá in easnamh? 65
Sort your stuff!.......................... 66
Who? When? Where? Quiz 68
Monster Maths 69
The Friend Books.......................70
Dear! 73
Puzail 74
Draw! 75
That's funny! 76
Tarraing 77
Time it! 78
Answers/Freagraí 79

Get ready for Christmas!

Sing and dance your way to Christmas with our seasonal song quiz. We've given you clues for the missing word in each Christmas song title. Can you figure them all out?

1. Fairytale of _ _ _ York (It's not old!)
2. All I Want for Christmas is _ _ _ (It's not me, it's…)
3. The _ _ _ _ _ _ Days of Christmas (Not eleven and not thirteen.)
4. _ _ _ _ Christmas (Not this Christmas or next Christmas!)
5. Santa Claus is Coming to _ _ _ _ (He's also making a list and checking it twice…)
6. _ _ _ _ _ _ _ _ _ _ Christmastime (Put 'Simply having a…' before this and you should get it!)
7. I Wish it Could be Christmas _ _ _ _ _ Day (Not on just one day…)
8. Merry Christmas _ _ _ _ _ _ _ _ _ (All the people!)
9. Driving _ _ _ _ for Christmas (Not driving to someone else's house!)
10. Rockin' Around the Christmas _ _ _ _ (Don't rock too close to it or you might get a pine needle in your bottom!)
11. Let it Snow! Let it Snow! Let it _ _ _ _ ! (Third time lucky)
12. _ _ _ _ _ _ the Snowman (Well, it's not 'Warmy the Snowman'…)
13. _ _ _ _ _ Christmas (Not a colourful colour!)
14. It's the Most Wonderful Time of the _ _ _ _ (Rhymes with 'near')
15. Have Yourself a _ _ _ _ _ Little Christmas (Rhymes with 'berry')

16. _____ and Wine (Don't stand under it unless you want a peck on the cheek!)

17. I Want a _____ for Christmas. (Somebody wants a big, mud-loving African animal for Christmas!)

18. When a _____ is Born (If you are in 3rd or 4th class, you are one!)

19. _____ the Red-Nosed Reindeer (No clue – it's too easy!)

20. _____ Wonderland (The singer is walking in one.)

21. It's Beginning to Look a Lot Like _____ (The answer's not 'Easter'!)

22. The Little _____ Boy (pa rum pum pum pum)

23. We ____ You a Merry Christmas (Rhymes with 'fish')

24. _____ Bells (No clue here either – this one's easy too!)

25. ____ the Herald Angels Sing (An old word for 'listen' – rhymes with 'dark')

26. _____ Night (Not the night you have your noisy Christmas party!)

27. The _____ and the Ivy (A prickly one!)

28. Deck the _____ (... with boughs of the answer to 27.)

29. Here Comes Santa _____ (If you don't know his name by now, there's no hope for you...)

30. Do They Know It's _____ ? (When you get your *Parade* annual!)

Answers on page 79

That's funny!

How much does it cost Santa to park his sleigh?
Nothing, it's on the house!

Why can you never tell a joke about pizza?
It would be too cheesy!

What is it called when a snowman loses his temper?
A meltdown!

What did one wall say to the other?
I'll meet you at the corner!

Where do boats go when they're sick?
To the dock!

What kind of car does an egg drive?
A yolkswagen!

How do you make 7 even?
Take away the s!

Why did Santa Claus get a parking ticket on Christmas Eve?
He left his sleigh in a snow parking zone!

Have you ever tried to catch a fog?
I tried yesterday but I mist!

What do you call a lazy baby kangaroo?
A pouch potato!

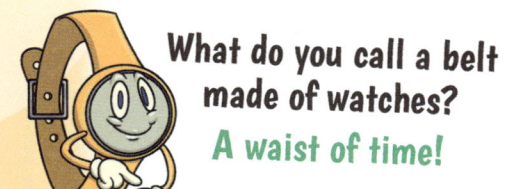

What do you call a belt made of watches?
A waist of time!

Do you want to hear a joke about paper?
Never mind, it's tearable!

What do you call someone with no body and no nose?
Nobody Knows!

What kind of music should you listen to while fishing?
Something catchy!

What does a librarian use to go fishing?
A bookworm!

What's the best way to watch a fishing competition?
Live stream!

How many storm troopers does it take to change a lightbulb?
None! Because they are all on the dark side …

What's the best air to breathe if you want to be rich?
Billionaire!

How did the barber win the race?
He knew a shortcut!

What invention allows us to see through walls?
Windows!

7

SANTA SCIENCE

N-ICE TRICK!

Get it ready!

A glass of water A piece of thread
An ice cube Salt

Try it!

1. Float an ice cube in a glass of water.
2. Ask someone if they can lift the ice cube out of the water with the piece of thread.
3. Wait until they give up!
4. Lay the piece of thread across the top of the ice cube.
5. Sprinkle some salt over the ice cube.
6. Wait a few seconds ...
7. Lift the thread carefully and the ice cube should be stuck to it!

Explain it!

The salt made the top of the ice cube melt a bit. Then the water washed the salt away. When the top of the cube was frozen again, the thread stuck to it!

DID YOU KNOW?

Plant stems draw water up from the ground. If the water in the stem freezes, it can cause tiny cracks in the stem. Then, if the air is cold, but the water in the ground isn't frozen, water drawn up the stem from the ground escapes through the cracks and freezes. Frozen ribbons of ice crystals form and look like flower petals. They are called frost flowers.

UPSIDE-DOWN WATER

Get it ready!
A glass
Water
A piece of card that is bigger than the top of the glass

Try it!
1. Fill the glass with water right to the very top.
2. Very carefully place the card over the top of the glass. Don't spill any water!
3. There should be no space for air in the glass, just water.
4. Put the palm of your hand flat on the card and slowly turn the glass upside down.
5. Carefully take away your hand!

Explain it!
The water can't push the card away as the air pushing against the outside of the card is stronger. You might need to try this one a few times to get it right. Always do this trick over the sink just in case!

STRIPY ICE!

Making stripy ice cubes takes time but it is worth the wait! The idea is to freeze each colour layer one at a time until you've built up a stack of colours.

Get it ready!
Food colouring
Water
An ice cube tray or other freezable container

IDEAS!
Make red and green striped ice cubes for your Christmas party.
Make ice cubes in your team colours.

Try it!
1. Pour your first colour into your tray or container so it covers the bottom.
2. Pop it into the freezer for about an hour to freeze.
3. Pour the next colour and refreeze for an hour.

Repeat colours or use different colours until you have reached the top of the container and the whole container is frozen. You can decide on how many layers and how many colours based on how much food colouring you have. The thickness of the layers depends on the size of your container.

Remember, be careful using food colouring as it stains easily. You don't need much of it to colour the water.

Make it!
Let's decorate!

You will need:
- A paper square (cut up a white or coloured A4 sheet)
- Glue or sticky tape
- Scissors

What you do:

1. Turn the first square so the points are north, south, east and west.

2. Fold up the bottom point up to top point and press the fold.

3. Fold the left side over to the right side as shown and press the fold.

4. Use scissors to cut three lines in the triangle as shown. Look closely at the length of the lines in the picture.

5. Unfold carefully.

6. Join both sides of the smallest inside square and stick them together.

7. Skip the next square. Join both sides of the third square and stick them together.

8. Turn it over. Join both sides of the second square and stick them together.

9. Join both sides of the largest outside square and stick them together.

10. Attach a ribbon loop to the top of your decoration to hang on your tree or repeat steps 1-9 for 5 more squares of paper, stick them together to make a snowflake.

Ideas!
Add sparkle by brushing on a little glitter glue.
Try making a smaller version to glue onto card to make a 3-D Christmas card.

Christmas cone tree

YOU WILL NEED

- PINE CONE
- GREEN AND WHITE ACRYLIC PAINTS
- BEADS
- KNITTING YARN
- CLAY PLASTICINE
- GLUE GLUE GUN

PINE CONE CHRISTMAS TREE

Idea!
Make one of these for each of your dinner guests and use it to decorate your Christmas dinner table.

Remember...
Pinecones should be cleaned before using them for crafts. Some people soak them in vinegar and water and some people bake them in the oven. Ask an adult to help you look up a way of doing this online.

Guess who?

Look at each face and name below. After two minutes, cover the faces and read the clues on page 13 to see if you can remember who is who!

Gus	Billy	Bobbi	Captain

Pearl	Sonny	Jack	Mavy

Charlie	Rebecca	Barry	Shay

Harry	Pat	Ms O

12

1. I tuck my hair under my chef's hat. My name is _____.
2. I look good in my shades. My name is _____.
3. I am wearing a navy shirt with a white collar. My name is _____.
4. I am completely bald. My name is _____.
5. I love the colour purple. My name is _____.
6. I wear glasses and my hair is a bit mad. My name is _____.
7. I wear my yellow hat when it's sunny. My name is _____.
8. I always wear a baseball cap. My name is _____.
9. I have long, straight, ginger hair. My name is _____.
10. I wear an eyepatch. My name is _____.
11. I have long, wavy, brown hair. My name is _____.
12. I have long hair and stubble. My name is _____.
13. I have a black fringe and am wearing red lipstick. My name is _____.
14. I wear my collar up on my jacket. My name is _____.
15. My chin has hair, but my head is bare. My name is _____.

Now, uncover page 12 and see if you remembered them all! Were there any clues in the names?

Science & Nature Quiz

1. How many legs does a spider have?
2. What tree does the acorn seed come from?
3. What are the two holes in your nose called?
4. What does a meteorologist study?
5. How many horns did a triceratops have?
6. What do pandas mostly eat?
7. In what part of your body would you find your pupil?
8. At what temperature (in degrees Celsius) does water freeze?
9. What part of your skeleton protects your brain?
10. Is the sun a star or a planet?
11. Is an ophthalmologist an eye doctor or an ear doctor?
12. Is a shark a fish or a mammal?
13. After a volcano has erupted, what is the molten (melted) rock called?
14. The Great Barrier Reef is found off the coast of which country?
15. What gemstone is used in most engagement rings?

Check your answers on page 79.

There were 15 questions. I knew _____ answers which means I learned _____ new things!

Puzail

Aimsigh deich rud atá i bhfolach sa phictiúr. Cuir tic sna boscaí nuair a aimsíonn tú iad.

An bhfaca tú éan i bhfolach sa leabharlann?

Ainmnigh an t-éan! Chonaic mé _____.

Freagraí ar leathanach 79

15

Little Puds!

What you need:

- 50g crisped rice cereal
- 30g chopped raisins
- 100g milk chocolate
- 2 tablespoons crunchy peanut butter
- 50g butter
- 30g mini marshmallows
- 80g white chocolate
- Ready-made icing holly leaves (or use food colouring with icing sugar and design your own)
- Small red sweets (or use food colouring with icing sugar and roll your own)
- Cling film
- Bowl
- Pot
- Egg cup
- Bun cases
- Tablespoon
- Wooden spoon

What you do:

1. Put the rice cereal and raisins into a bowl.
2. Break the milk chocolate (the brown chocolate) into pieces.
3. Put the butter, milk chocolate, peanut butter and marshmallows into a small pot.
4. Ask an adult to help you heat the pot on a medium to low heat.
5. Keep stirring until the chocolate and butter have melted but the marshmallows are only starting to melt.
6. Pour the chocolate mix into the rice cereal mix and stir gently until well mixed.
7. Line an egg cup with cling film.
8. Put about a tablespoon of the mixture into the egg cup and press it down firmly.
9. Then take it out and peel off the cling film.
10. Put the pudding into a bun case, flat side down.
11. Do this with the rest of the mixture.
12. Put the puddings in the fridge to chill until they are firm.
13. Ask an adult to help you melt the white chocolate in bowl over a saucepan of barely simmering water or in the microwave.
14. Spoon a little white chocolate over the top of each pudding.
15. Let the chocolate set in the fridge for a couple of minutes.
16. Decorate the top with icing holly, using a blob of chocolate to stick them on if necessary.

Ideas!

Make puds out of chocolate truffles or scoops of chocolate ice cream.

Decorate chocolate profiteroles to make them look like mini puddings.

Decorate a cupcake, muffin or chocolate teacake to look like a pudding.

17

The Jaguar Man

1 Alan Robert Rabinowitz was born in Brooklyn, New York in 1953. He was a smart kid with a love of nature, but he had a problem ...

2 When he spoke, Alan's words would get stuck. He knew the words but couldn't get them to flow into sentences. This caused him to repeat sounds while he was speaking. He was told he had a stutter, which is also called a stammer.

3 Poor Alan! Teachers put him in classes for kids with learning difficulties, but he had no difficulty learning. Doctors put him in treatments, but these just made him think that something was wrong with him. He felt adults didn't understand his problem, so he stopped speaking to them and spoke to his pets ...

4 Alan was lonely and confused. When he got home after a hard day at school, he would go into the clothes closet in his bedroom and sit with his pet chameleon, snake, turtle, hamster and gerbil. Then Alan would talk to the animals and tell them all about his day and his dream to speak up for them some day.

5 And it wasn't just his pets. At the zoo he spent hours watching the big cats. His favourite cat – an old jaguar – would come right over to him. Alan started whispering to it and his words came easily. He could chat to the cat! He promised the jaguar that if he ever found his voice in the human world, he would use it to help big cats.

6 And Alan did find his voice! With the help of a speech clinic, he trained himself to overcome his stammer. He could finally communicate all the words that he had been trying to say. He was 18, ready to go to university and ready to study the animals he loved.

I love animals!
Especially jaguars!
I'll need more books!
...Look, a kitten!

18

7 At first, Alan studied black bears, raccoons and bats. Then the real adventures began! Alan travelled to jungles, rainforests and mountains. He trekked to one of the most isolated parts of the world in Myanmar and discovered the world's smallest deer. It is called the leaf muntjac or leaf deer.

8 But the big cats still needed a voice. In 2006, Alan helped set up Panthera, an organisation that protects the world's wild cats and where they live. He mapped **habitats** and recorded damage caused by development. He used his voice to persuade governments to provide land to **preserve** the wild cats. He used his voice to save ecosystems.

9 For his final project, Alan worked for over a decade to protect jaguars. Through his work, he discovered that there was no **subspecies** of jaguar so all jaguars from Arizona to Argentina were connected by their habitat. He decided to open the world's first jaguar **sanctuary** in Belize, a country south of Mexico.

10 One day, Alan was walking in the sanctuary when he spotted tracks from a large jaguar. He followed them. It was getting dark when he turned to see the jaguar behind him. He thought it would attack, but it just sat down and looked at him. Eventually, the cat growled, stood up and walked away and Alan looked into its eyes and whispered, 'Thank you.'

11 Sadly, Alan died in 2018. This amazing **conservationist** and big cat expert understood how wildlife, humans and habitats all relate to each other, and the importance of those relationships. He started off with no voice but became the voice of wildcats everywhere.

Wildlife word watch:
Preserve: To keep something safe from harmful change.
Sanctuary: A restricted area to protect natural resources like animals or plants.
Conservationist: A person who works to preserve and mind the environment and wildlife.
Habitat: The place where a plant or animal naturally lives and grows.
Subspecies: Animals that look like another animal but live in a different place.

Check it out!
Read or listen to Alan's picture book *A Boy and a Jaguar*. Ask an adult to help you find it on YouTube.

19

Design

Big cat facts!

- There are 40 species of wild cats in the world.
- There are seven big cat species: lions, tigers, jaguars, leopards, snow leopards, cheetahs and pumas.
- The panther family includes five of these: lion, tiger, jaguar, leopard and snow leopard.
- Pumas and cheetahs are often called 'big cats' as they weigh over 50 kgs, but they have different characteristics and evolved much later than the true big cats.
- A black panther is not a different type of cat. A black panther is just a leopard or a jaguar with black fur!

Design your own wild cat with unusual markings, strange colours and a funny tail! Give your cat a name.

I am going to call my cat creation a _____.

Dathaigh

Dathaigh an pictiúr seo de iaguar lena coileán.

MONSTER Maths

Help Mookie figure out the number for each robot and android. Remember if you get stuck on a line, the next line in that puzzle might help you solve it!

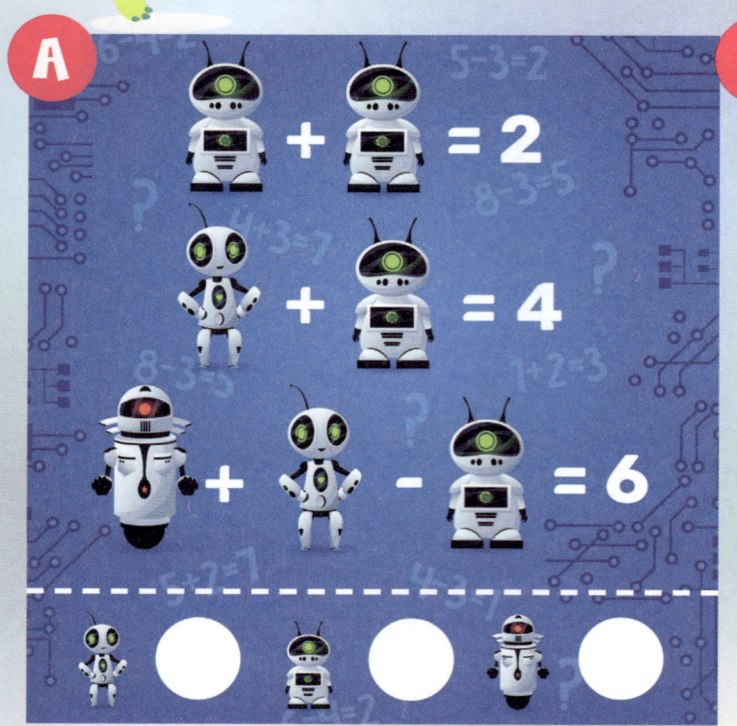

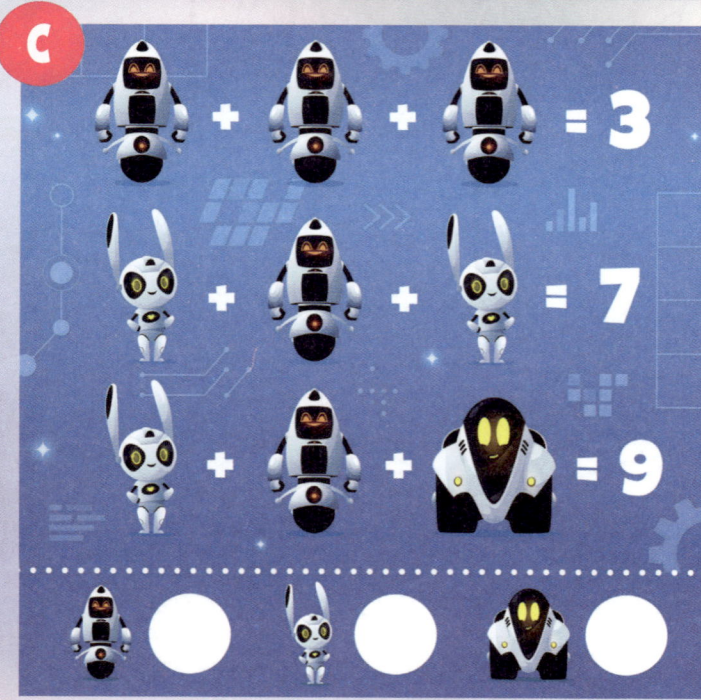

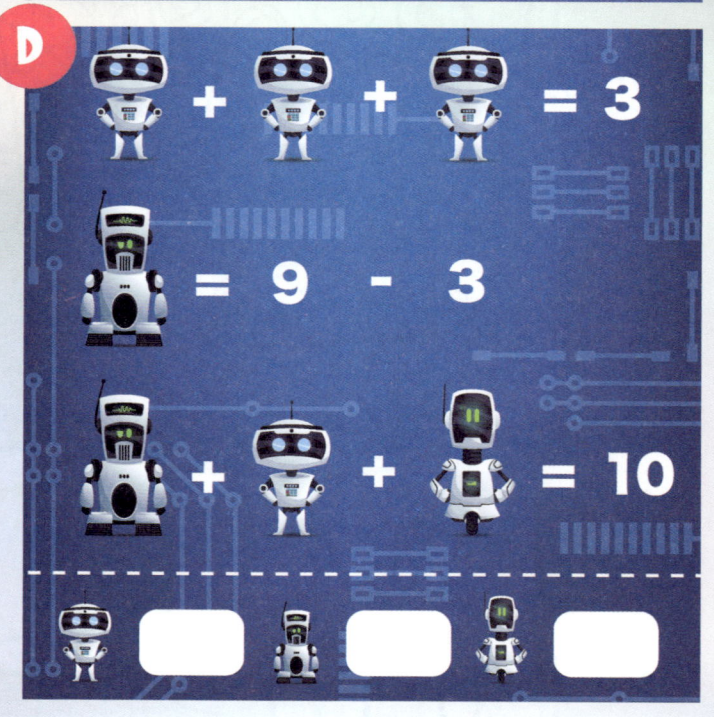

A
- 🤖 + 🤖 = 2
- 🤖 + 🤖 = 4
- 🤖 + 🤖 − 🤖 = 6

B
- 🤖 + 🤖 + 🤖 = 3
- 🤖 + 🤖 + 🤖 = 6
- 🤖 + 🤖 − 🤖 = 5

C
- 🤖 + 🤖 + 🤖 = 3
- 🤖 + 🤖 + 🤖 = 7
- 🤖 + 🤖 + 🤖 = 9

D
- 🤖 + 🤖 + 🤖 = 3
- 🤖 = 9 − 3
- 🤖 + 🤖 + 🤖 = 10

Are robots and androids the same thing?
Androids are robots that are more like human beings in how they look and how they do things.

Answers on page 79

Tangled!

Starting at the coloured bows, trace to the end of each tail and colour the bow in the same colour.

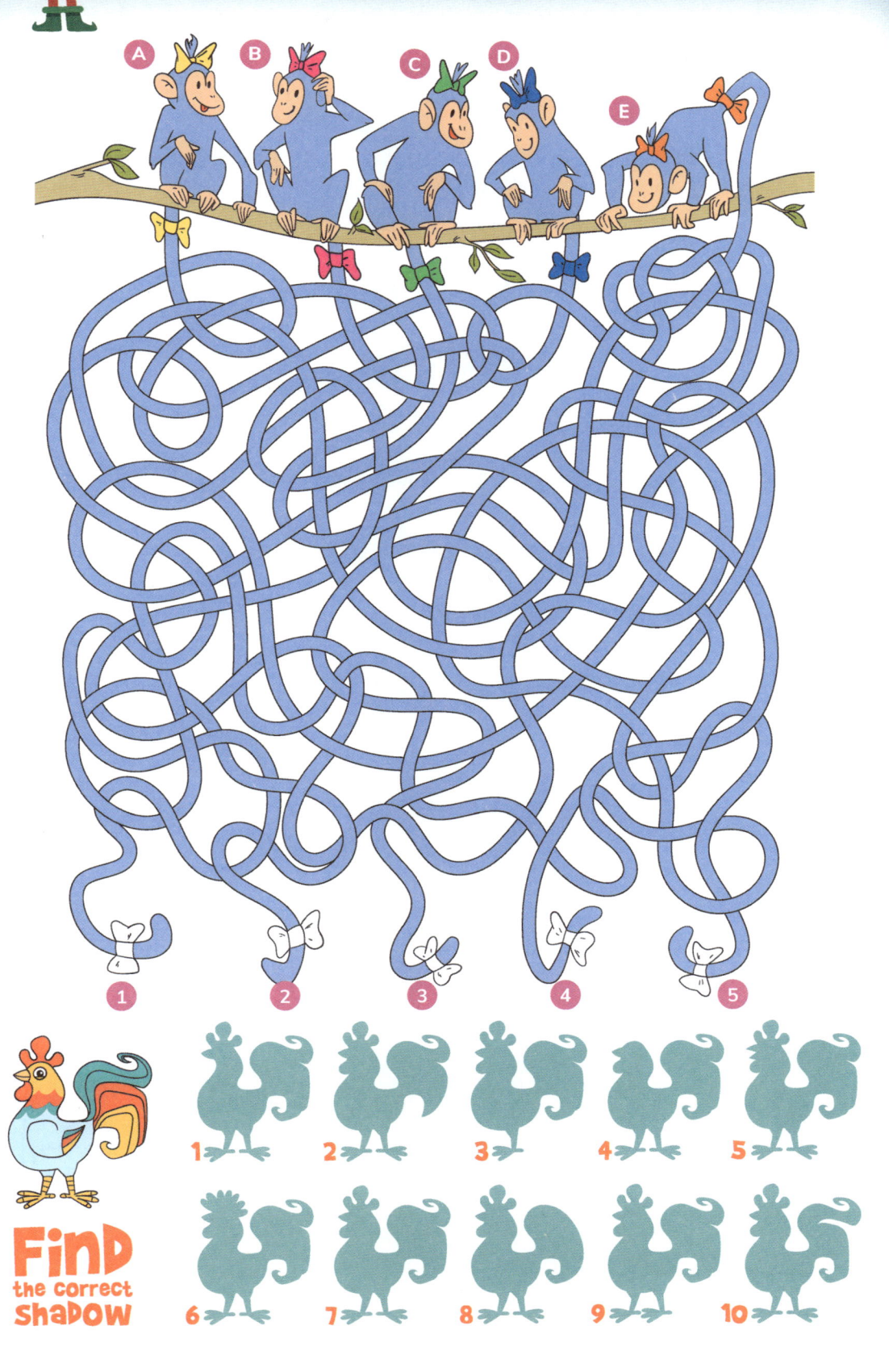

A B C D E

1 2 3 4 5

Find the correct shadow

1 2 3 4 5

6 7 8 9 10

Answers on page 79

23

Sports & Hobbies Quiz

1. How many cards in a deck of cards?

2. For which sea sport do you stand on a board?

3. What is the name of the stick with a reel used for fishing?

4. What are the long black and white buttons on a piano called?

5. What is the value of the red ball in snooker?

6. In ballet, what is a full turn on one foot called?

7. What are the three main sports of the GAA?

8. How many points is a goal worth in hurling?

9. What do swimmers wear on their eyes in the water?

10. For which pastime would you need two needles and a ball of wool?

11. What type of puzzle involves fitting different shapes together to form a picture?

12. What is used to steer a boat when sailing?

13. What colour jersey does the leader of the Tour de France wear?

14. In athletics, what is the name of the spear-like object thrown by athletes?

15. When playing guitar, what is the little bit of plastic used to pluck the strings called?

Check your answers on page 79.

There were 15 questions. I knew _____ answers which means I learned _____ new things!

Crosfhocal

Oibrigh amach an focal a nascann gach sraith pictiúr. Líon isteach an crosfhocal.

Síos

1.
3.
4.
5.
7.

Trasna

2.
4.
6.

Freagraí ar leathanach 79

LOOK AGAIN!

Cropped pictures, turned images or just close-up photos. What are these things?

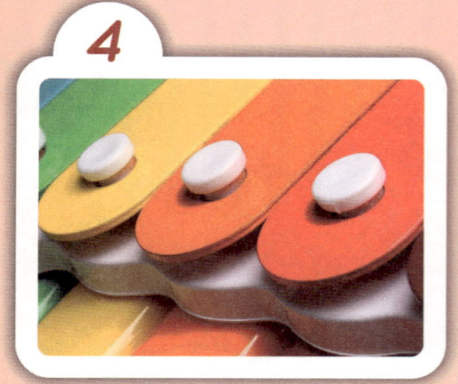

1
2
3
4
5
6
7
8
9
10
11
12

ANSWERS ON PAGE 79

27

A Smash Hit!

1 Nobody knows for sure where piñatas originated, but they have been around for about 800 years.

2 It is believed that on his travels to China, Marco Polo saw farmers hang up paper sculptures stuffed with seeds. They hit them with sticks to make the seeds scatter as a symbol of a good harvest.

3 Marco brought the idea home to Italy. Italians began filling clay cooking pots called *pignattas* with treats to hang and hit as part of their Christian ceremonies.

4 Later, the Spanish adopted this tradition with slightly different clay pots and the Spanish spelling *piñata*. They started decorating their pots with colourful ribbons.

5 In Mexico in the 1600s, monks made a piñata with cones representing the seven deadly sins. Whacking the piñata represented whacking evil out of the world! The treats inside symbolised rewards for good behaviour.

6 This developed into the Mexican festival *La Posadas* celebrating the nativity. At the end of the festival procession on Christmas Eve, when Mary and Joseph arrived at the stable, they hung a clay donkey with sweets inside.

7 Mexicans started decorated their piñatas with colourful paper fringes. Eventually, people realised that a clay pot breaking over the heads of children wasn't a great idea, so they started making papier-mâché piñatas.

8 This meant that piñatas could be made into any shape. And if they could look like anything, they could be used for anything! Piñatas are now sold for any celebration where people gather for a party across the world.

How to play piñata ...

How you play piñata depends on where the party is being held, and on the number and age of the players. Really young children should have a lower piñata filled with suitable treats and a lighter, shorter stick. Whether you spin and blindfold each player depends on the child.

For older kids, the piñata should be hung on a string from the ceiling (if the party is indoors) or a tree (if outdoors).

During his or her turn, each child is blindfolded and given a stick to hit the piñata. Decide on the number of strikes each child can make in their turn (usually three).

If you are spinning players, decide on the number of times each player is to be spun before you start the game (usually three).

Everyone should line up for their turn and be careful to avoid getting bashed by a dizzy blindfolded kid with a stick!

¡FELIZ NAVIDAD!

Did you know ...

In some countries, they have a special song that they sing when a player starts their turn and when the song is over, the stick gets passed to the next player.

There are also piñatas with a special panel in the bottom. Ribbons are attached to the panel and left hanging from the bottom of the piñata. Instead of hitting the piñata with a stick, each child is given a ribbon to hold. After a countdown, the children all pull their ribbons at the same time to release the treats from the piñata.

What's in the piñata?

Unscramble the names of the treats to find out!

colchoate insco _____ _____

plillpoos _____

estews _____

beblub mug _____ _____

nimi thococlae rsba ____ _____ ____

Answers on page 79

Dathaigh

Dathaigh na milseáin ón bpiñata!

30

Puzail

Aimsigh dhá rud déag atá i bhfolach sa phictiúr.

Cén píosa atá in easnamh ó gach earra?

Freagraí ar leathanach 79

31

Aimsigh na Difríochtaí

Aimsigh deich ndifríocht atá ann idir an dá phictiúr.

Aimsigh cúig dhifríocht atá ann idir an dá phictiúr.

Aimsigh deich ndifríocht atá ann idir an dá phictiúr.

Aimsigh cúig dhifríocht atá ann idir an dá phictiúr.

Freagraí ar leathanach 79

33

How many?

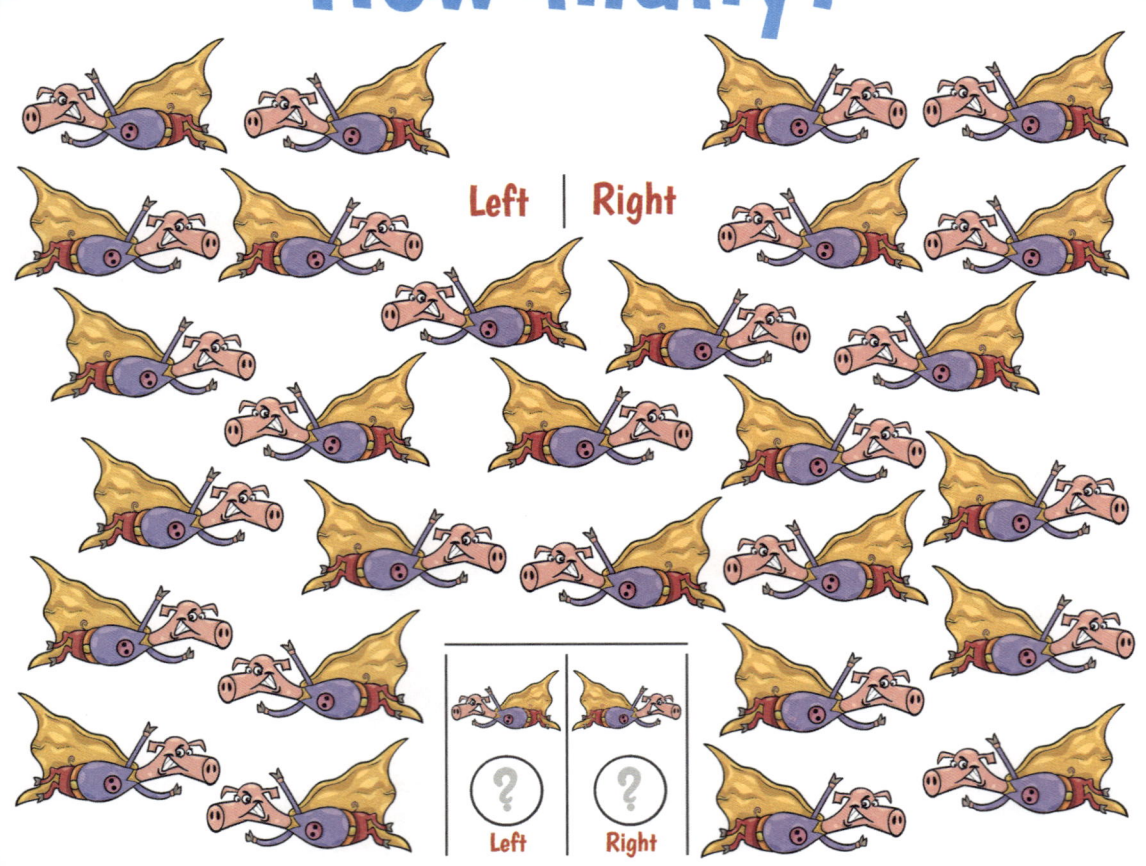

Left | Right

Cé mhéad?

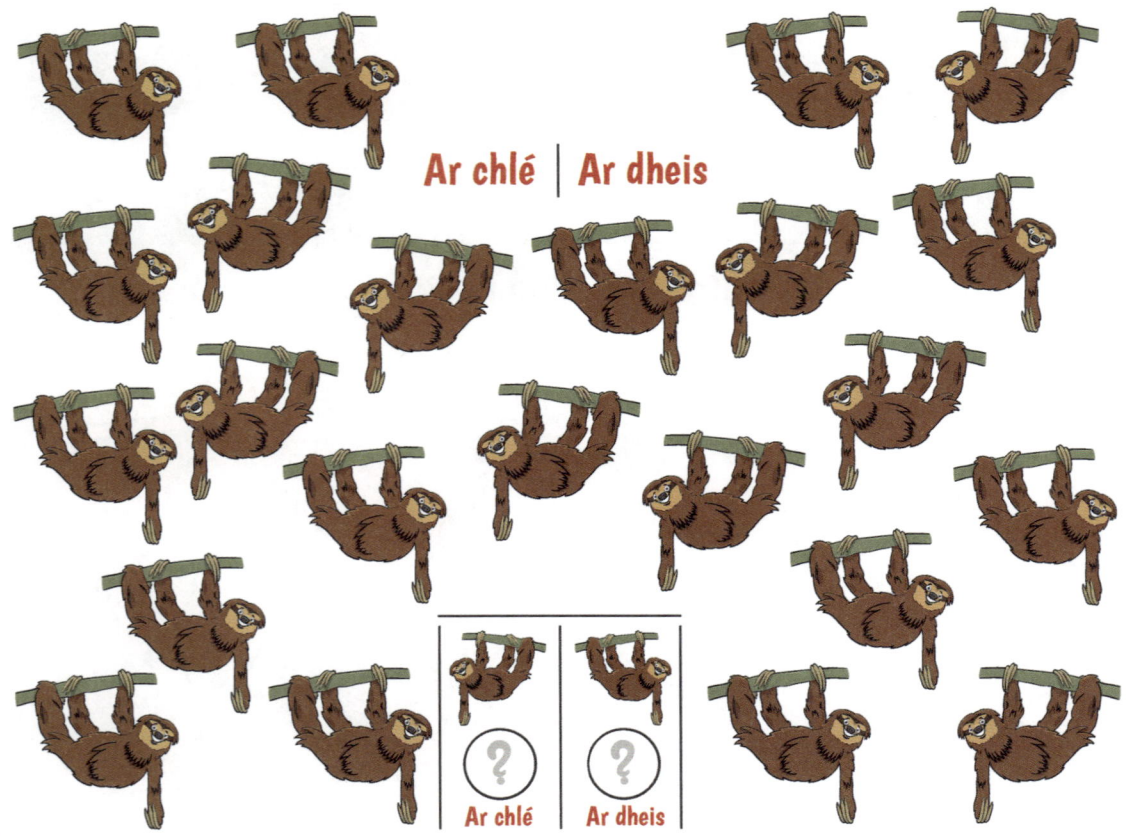

Ar chlé | Ar dheis

Freagraí ar leathanach 79

Winter Quiz

1. Name the three winter months.

2. For which winter sport are both feet strapped to one board?

3. What type of gloves have one part for your thumb and one for your fingers?

4. I am long, usually made from wool and I keep your neck warm. What am I?

5. What is the name of the red-breasted bird we see in winter?

6. In which tasty winter drink do we put marshmallows?

7. What do we call the tiny ice crystals that form on the ground on a cold morning?

8. What date is 'Little Christmas' or 'Nollaig na mBan'?

9. What is a hedgehog's long winter sleep called?

10. What is traditionally used for a snowman's nose?

11. Coniferous trees do not lose their leaves in winter. They are e_____.

12. What is spread on our frozen roads to make them less slippery?

13. Which winter month is named after the Roman god Janus?

14. What date is Christmas Eve?

15. What is the name of the calendar that counts down to Christmas?

Check your answers on page 79.

There were 15 questions. I knew _____ answers which means I learned _____ new things!

That's funny!

Where do Santa's elves go swimming?
The North pool!

Why does Santa go down the chimney?
Because it soots him!

What do you call a girl in the middle of a tennis court?
Annette!

Why should you never use a blunt pencil?
Because it's pointless!

What do you give a scientist with bad breath?
An experi-mint!

What do you call a herd of sheep falling down a hill?
A lambslide!

What do you call a medieval lamp?
A knight light!

What do cows like to read?
Cattle-logs!

Why was the broom late?
It over-swept!

What type of person sells perfume?
Someone with lots of scents!

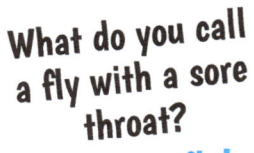

What do you call a fly with a sore throat?
A hoarse fly!

What day of the week are most twins born on?
Twos-day!

What is fast and tastes like potatoes?
A rocket chip!

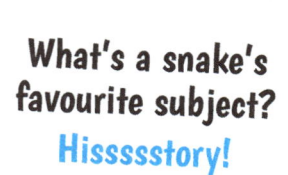

What's a snake's favourite subject?
Hisssssstory!

Where does a rat go when it has a toothache?
To the rodentist!

What do you call a dinosaur fart?
A blast from the past!

What is blue and easy to lift?
Light blue!

Why did the lion cross the road?
To get to the other pride!

37

Chocolate Chipping!

Creating a sculpture out of chocolate can be as easy or as difficult as you like. Have a go at creating a chocolatey masterpiece!

What type of chocolate will I use?

Any chocolate will do! We recommend that you look out for the Fairtrade logo when you buy chocolate. The Fairtrade Foundation is an international organisation that helps workers and farmers who produce chocolate in poorer countries receive a fair wage for their work. Buying Fairtrade chocolate means you are helping them too. Look for the logo!

How do I start?

First, you need to temper the chocolate. Tempering is the gradual heating of chocolate to stop it cracking when you work with it. A microwave works best. It is important to get an adult to help here. Place the chocolate in the microwave for 30 second bursts. Stir after each burst. This helps distribute the temperature in the chocolate. If the melted chocolate has a few lumps left, keep stirring until you're left with smooth chocolate.

How will I know it is ready?

Stick the end of a teaspoon in the melted chocolate. If the chocolate on the spoon sets within three to five minutes at room temperature, it's ready to use.

What can I do with it?

Use your imagination, but also use greaseproof paper to stop it sticking! Create shapes, then let them set. Ask an adult to help you carve your chocolate to make features. Use toothpicks to add details. The great thing about working with chocolate is that it is like clay, so if you don't like what you've made, you can just reheat the chocolate and have another go! If you plan to decorate your creations with sprinkles, dried fruit or nuts, do this before the chocolate sets so they stick better.

Ideas!

Set a lollipop stick in the centre and turn your shape into a chocolate lolly.

Make hot chocolate cubes. Fill an ice tray with melted chocolate, pop a lollipop stick in each cube and let them set at room temperature. Swirl them into hot milk to make a warm chocolatey drink. Add marshmallows, a candy cane and whipped cream to make a special treat!

Try using moulds or different types of chocolate to create more difficult sculptures. Ask an adult to help you look up suitable chocolate sculpting tutorials on YouTube.

Did you know?

Chocolate sculptors made a chocolate sculpture of the actor Timothée Chalamet dressed as the character Willy Wonka. It took five weeks and around 100 kg of chocolate to make! It was a really heavy sculpture and very difficult to move. On one journey, a finger and a hand broke off. Yikes! However, because chocolate can be melted down and stuck back on, they soon had a complete Wonka again.

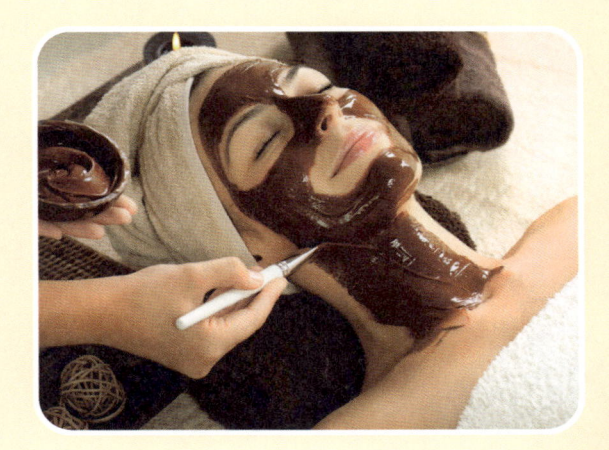

Chocolate can be used as a type of beauty therapy. Good quality dark chocolate is thought to be useful for soothing your skin. It contains vegetable proteins, vitamins and minerals. You'll need to clean your skin after the chocolate facial has done its job or you'll be licking your face all day!

There are chocolate museums all over the world telling the history of chocolate and displaying some amazing chocolate sculptures. Look at these sculptures of famous landmarks in Istanbul in Turkey made from white and milk chocolate. Look how thin the chocolate is in the bridge!

You could meet characters from a fairy tale like Hansel and Gretel. Imagine if you met a life-size chocolate version of yourself!

Sculptures like these are not meant for eating and will last a long time if kept at the right temperature.

Cocoa beans are the main ingredient in making chocolate. The ideal climate for growing cocoa is hot, rainy and tropical. Cocoa is grown in Africa, Asia and Latin America.

Puzail

Cé mhéad glas atá ann sa phictiúr? Dathaigh iad!

Cé mhéad? _____

Aimsigh an scáth ceart don eochair órga.

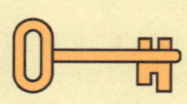

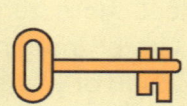

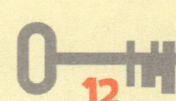

1 2 3
4 5 6
7 8 9
10 11 12

Puzzles

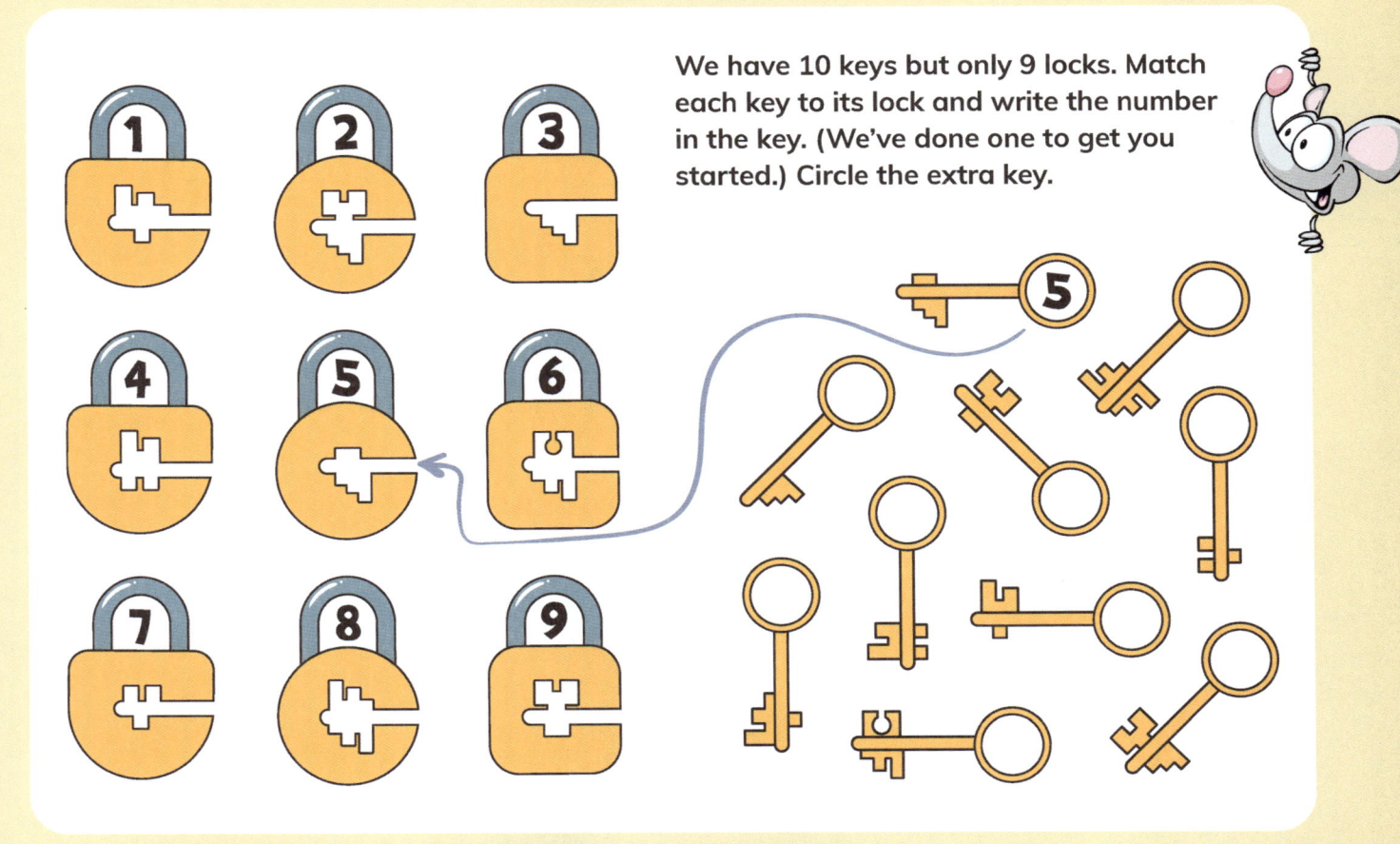

We have 10 keys but only 9 locks. Match each key to its lock and write the number in the key. (We've done one to get you started.) Circle the extra key.

Match the sum on each lock to an answer key.

1+6   7−2   3+5

5   8   3   7   2   9

6+3   8−6   6−3

Answers on page 79/80

FÉACH ARÍS!

Cad atá ann i ngach ceann de na grianghraif seo? Seans go mbeidh ort breathnú arís! An bhfuil téama ann?

1
2
3
4
5
6
7
8
9
10
11
12

FREAGRAÍ AR
LEATHANACH 80

What a load of nonsense!

Nonsense poetry is poetry that is a little bit silly. It often rhymes and is usually funny. Limericks are a type of nonsense verse. Did you ever try to write a limerick?

A poet called Edward Lear wrote lots of limericks. He wrote a whole book of them called *A Book of Nonsense*. One of the best-known limericks from his book is this one:

> There was an Old Man with a beard,
> Who said, 'It is just as I feared!
> Two Owls and a Hen,
> Four Larks and a Wren
> Have all built their nests in my beard!'

Imagine it ... what a crazy idea!

Look at the way Edward used the same word at the end of the first and last line. This helps us recognise that the poem is a limerick.

What else makes this poem a limerick?

It has five lines.

> There was an Old Man with a beard
> Who said, 'It is just as I feared!
> Two Owls and a Hen,
> Four Larks and a Wren
> Have all built their nests in my beard!'

The third and fourth lines are shorter and rhyme.

The first, second and fifth lines are longer and rhyme.

The last line is funny!

44

Have a go at writing your own beard poem about Santa's beard. You can try writing a limerick if you like. Have a think about other words that rhyme with beard like weird, tiered, cheered and sheared. Remember, if you don't use the word 'beard' at the end of the first line, you don't have to find something to rhyme with it in the second!

Did you know?

Writers like Dr Seuss (who wrote *The Cat in the Hat* books) and Lewis Carroll (who wrote the *Alice in Wonderland* stories) also wrote nonsense poems. They used ordinary words in extraordinary ways. They also used extraordinary words in ordinary ways! When we play with words, mixing them up and creating new ones, things can get a bit ridiculous!

Puzzles

A Write the number for the missing piece in the circle. Cross off each coloured circle as you use it. We've done one for you!

1 2 3̸ 4 5 6 7 8 9 10

B Match two pieces each time to make 12 squares.

46

C Match the blocks to the building. We've put one together for you!

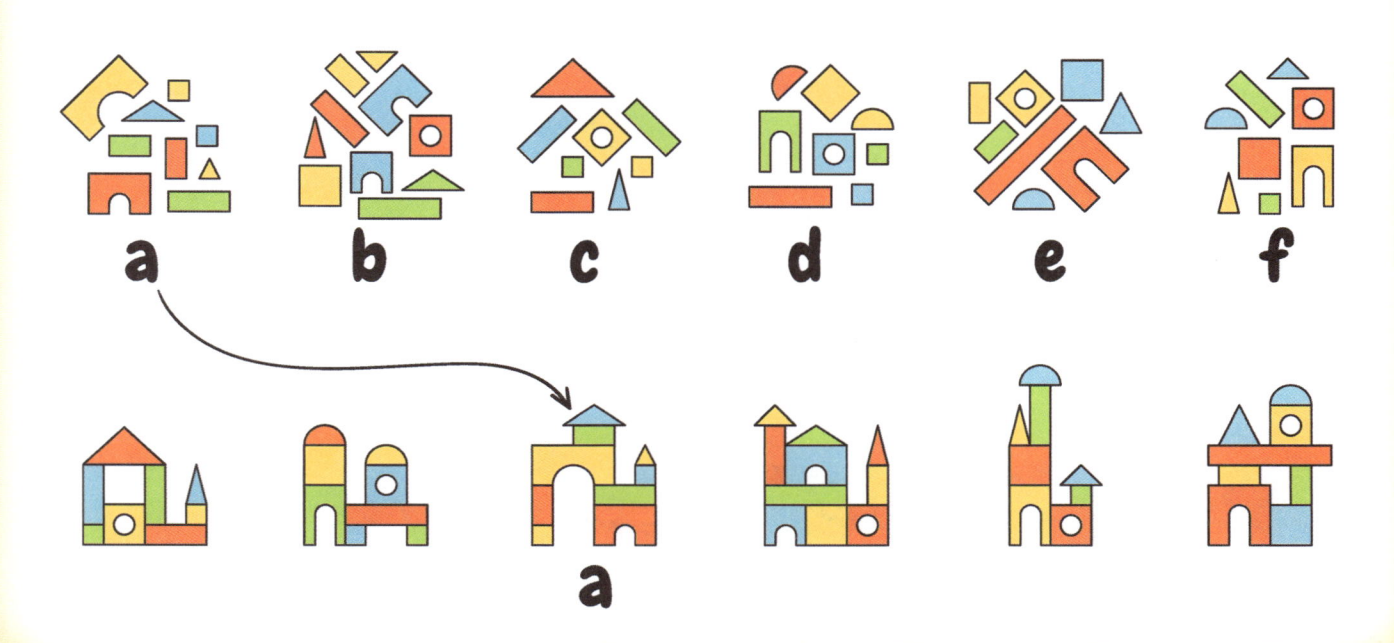

a   b   c   d   e   f

a

D Find the missing piece of pizza. We've found the first one for you!

A   B   C   D   E

A

What is Santa's favourite pizza topping?
Pepper-ho-ho-ho-ni!

Answers on page 80

47

Make it!

Have a go at making this festive decoration. You can make one to hang on your tree, or thread them onto a string to hang across the room. There are two items to make: a paper ball and a fan. Try making one of each first. Then decide which one you might like to make more of.

Fan

Step 1

Find the things you need: squares of paper (two different colours), scissors, a ruler, a pencil and a glue stick.

Step 2

Cut the square in half. Fold the half over top to bottom edge. Cut a rectangular section out of the side as shown.

Step 3

Unfold the piece of paper. Use a ruler to draw lines across as shown. Then fold like a fan until you have a strip.

Step 4

Fold the long side in half. Put glue along the edge. Glue the two halves together.

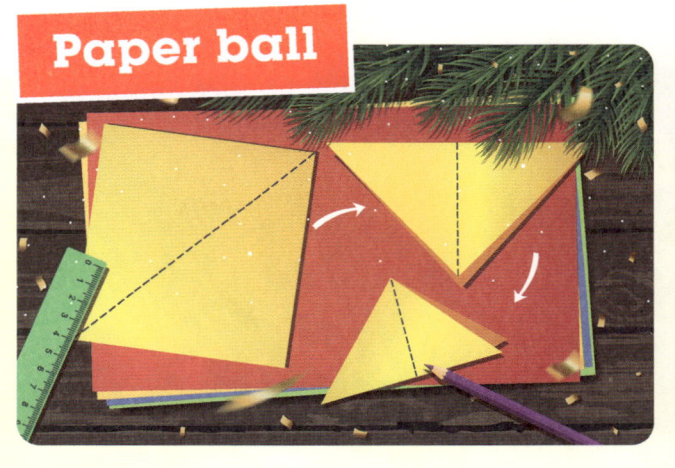

Paper ball

Step 5
Fold the square of paper diagonally. Then fold the triangle in half again. Fold it in half a third time.

Step 6
Cut the top of the folded triangle in a curve as shown.

Step 7
Use a ruler (or an adult!) to help you draw the outline shown in orange above. Carefully cut away the paper around the shape you've drawn. Open it out.

Step 8
Fold in arm 1 of the shape, then fold in arm 3. Glue them together at the circle. Repeat this with arms 5, 7, 2, 4, 6 and 8, in that order.

Step 9
String a ball onto the string, then a fan, then a ball, then a fan. You can make the decoration as long as you like by making more balls and fans.

And now you've made it!

Snow Business

So, when it comes to snow, here's some stuff you need to know!

How does a snowflake happen?
When it gets extremely cold high in the sky, a water droplet freezes onto pollen or dust particles. This forms an ice crystal. As the crystal falls to the ground, water vapour freezes onto it. This water vapour creates new crystals, and these make the snowflake.

Why do all snowflakes have six points or arms?
A snowflake is made of frozen water. Water is made up of hydrogen and oxygen atoms. Water has two hydrogen atoms and one oxygen atom (H_2O). The three atoms together are called a molecule. The molecule is a V shape. When water molecules freeze together, they make a hexagon shape with six sides.

As more water molecules stick to a forming snowflake, the shape does not change. The snowflake gets bigger but keeps its six sides.

Why is every snowflake different?
Each snowflake follows a slightly different path from the sky to the ground. This means that every snowflake travels through slightly different conditions in the atmosphere on the way down, so the water vapour freezes slightly differently on each one. It takes about an hour for a snowflake to reach the ground so a lot of shape shifting goes on as it falls.

Why is snow white?
News flash ... snow isn't actually white! Snow looks white as it falls from the clouds or collects on the ground, but it's actually translucent (nearly transparent). That's because snow is made up of tiny ice crystals that are almost see-through. It is light shining on the snowflake that makes it look white. The light bounces off all the little crystals in different directions. It is the same when we look at sugar or salt.

How to make the best snowballs

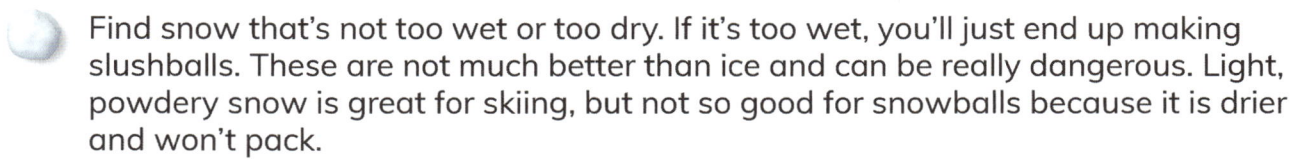

- Find snow that's not too wet or too dry. If it's too wet, you'll just end up making slushballs. These are not much better than ice and can be really dangerous. Light, powdery snow is great for skiing, but not so good for snowballs because it is drier and won't pack.

- Wear gloves, not mittens. It will be easier to shape the ball. Also less heat escapes from a mitten and you need a little heat to pack a snowball. The heat melts the surface of the snowball enough to help it pack.

- Go with the snow a few inches below the surface. This snow is already packed down by the surface layer, so you'll have less packing to do!

- Cup your hands, fill both of them with snow and bring your hands together. Rotate your hands as you press the snow into a ball shape. Don't press too hard at first or you'll crush the ball! Gradually build up the pressure, pressing a little harder each time as the ball gets a bigger.

- When you feel resistance from the snow as you pack, the snowball is ready. Stop pressing and start smoothing the snow into a perfect ball.

- Now, have some fun!

Find 5 differences.

Answers on page 80

SNOWBALL FIGHT

The air is crisp, it snowed all night.
There's going to be a snowball fight ...

        The winter sun is glinting bright.
        There's going to be a snowball fight ...

Our garden's covered, all is white.
There's going to be a snowball fight ...

        I'll pack the snow round nice and tight.
        There's going to be a snowball fight ...

Not too heavy, not too light.
There's going to be a snowball fight ...

        My pile is growing (what a height!)
        There's going to be a snowball fight ...

I'll throw each ball with all my might.
There's going to be a snowball fight ...

        I'll take aim and they'll take flight.
        There's going to be a snowball fight ...

My target will soon be in sight.
There's going to be a snowball fight ...

        I kinda pity my sister's plight.
        There's going to be a snowball fight ...

She'll get the most tremendous fright.
There's going to be a snowball fight ...

        Wait, there's something not quite right ...
        NO! *She* started the snowball fight!

The Snowman Café

Wait, till I tell you what happened
When I went to the Snowman Café
When a waiter came over to serve me
I asked, 'What's the soup of the day?'

'We've carrot soup today,' he said.
And he tipped the edge of his hat.
'Oh lovely, carrot's my favourite.
'I'll be having a bowl of that!'

The waiter wore gloves on his hands
So holding the tray was tricky
Maybe his twigs were a little bit cold
Or maybe his hands were sticky …

The soup came out all steaming hot
With a bread roll on a plate
And a little rectangle of butter
I thought, 'This is going to be great!'

I snapped my napkin over my lap
And quickly buttered my roll
I picked up my spoon to dip it in
Then, I looked in the bowl …

The soup was a funny colour,
But I shrugged and gave it a try
The carrots tasted funny, too,
And then, I let out a cry …

'Yuck, it's not carrot, it's mushroom!
It's not the right soup, can't you see?'
The snowman lifts it, sniffs it and says,
'Well, it smells like carrot to me!'

Souped up!
Simple Veggie Soup

What you need:
- 200g chopped vegetables such as onions, celery and carrots
- 300g potatoes, peeled and cubed
- 1 tbsp oil
- 700ml stock
- crème fraîche and fresh herbs, to serve

What you do:
1. Fry the vegetables and potatoes in a pan with the oil for a few minutes until they begin to soften.
2. Cover with the stock and simmer for 10-15 mins until the veg is tender.
3. Blend until smooth.
4. Season.
5. Serve with a dollop of crème fraîche and some fresh herbs.

carrot, cabbage, onion, eggplant, sunflower, corn, potato, tomato, chile, pepper, mushroom, wheat, beet, peas, cucumber, pumpkin, radish, broccoli, I love vegetables

Find all the healthy ingredients pictured in the wordsearch grid.

P	C	A	R	R	O	T	J	V	W	B	C	O	R	N
Y	B	U	G	V	C	U	C	U	M	B	E	R	S	A
R	A	D	I	S	H	G	F	N	H	P	B	W	Z	V
P	O	K	P	O	T	A	T	O	J	E	M	H	Q	J
E	I	I	J	O	N	I	O	N	N	P	E	A	S	R
G	W	S	V	O	N	L	T	I	N	P	F	C	L	J
G	H	U	H	Y	V	E	K	X	T	E	O	T	H	O
P	E	N	L	U	E	P	L	L	T	R	F	B	I	D
L	A	F	Y	B	M	U	S	H	R	O	O	M	R	P
A	T	L	L	U	P	Q	U	I	D	F	M	G	L	V
N	J	O	P	D	I	Y	Z	C	A	B	B	A	G	E
T	I	W	R	P	O	W	B	Y	U	D	F	L	T	Z
U	I	E	D	J	N	B	Z	S	E	R	L	O	R	O
W	B	R	O	C	C	O	L	I	L	C	H	I	L	I
E	B	L	J	N	X	Q	T	R	T	O	H	P	A	K

Look at the purple vegetable in the healthy foods list. What name do we usually use instead of eggplant? Unscramble the letters to find out.

R̶U̶G B E A N I E   A U _ _ _ _ _ _ _ _

Answers on page 80

55

General Knowledge Quiz

1. Which chess piece looks like a castle tower?
2. What are ballet, tap and hip-hop types of?
3. Which country has a maple leaf on its flag?
4. Name Winnie the Pooh's tiger friend.
5. What is the capital of Hungary?
6. Who was the god of sky and thunder and king of the gods in Greek mythology?
7. How many tentacles does a squid have?
8. Which actor does the voice of Po in the *Kung Fu Panda* movies?
9. What do Americans call an aubergine?
10. In Greek mythology, the god of the sea is called Poseidon. What is he called in Roman mythology?
11. In which movie does Ryan Gosling play a character called 'Ken'?
12. What are our big back teeth called?
13. What colour is a flamingo?
14. Which UK music artist had a hit with the song *Houdini*?
15. What is another name for the finger that you use to point at something?

Check your answers on page 80.

There were 15 questions. I knew _____ answers which means I learned _____ new things!

Tangled!

Start at the bottom of each bird's neck and follow it up. Write the same number at the top.

Find the correct shadow

FÉACH ARÍS!

Cad atá ann i ngach ceann de na grianghraif seo?
Seans go mbeidh ort breathnú arís!

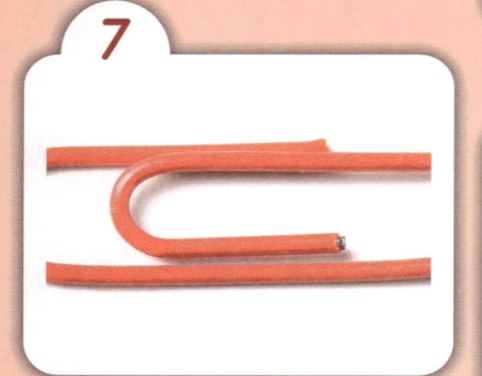

1

2

3

4

5

6

7

8

9

10

11

12

58

FREAGRAÍ AR
LEATHANACH 80

Something for everyone!

We are so proud of all our Irish athletes who competed in both the European Championships and the Olympics this year. What a great year for athletics in Ireland! But what exactly is the sport of athletics? Athletics is basically organised running, jumping and throwing. There are about 365 athletics clubs in Ireland with over 66,500 members. That's a lot of running, jumping and throwing going on around the country! Read on to find out about the different events in athletics; there really is something for everyone …

Running!

Whether you are a sprinter or more of a slow-and-steady jogger, there is a running distance for you in athletics. The short and fast track races start at 60 metres and go up to 10,000 metres (eek!). Or, if running really fast around in circles is not for you, try road racing or cross-country. Road races start at a mile (a bit longer than a kilometre) and if you're old enough and trained enough, you can run a marathon!

If you feel that running is a bit full on, race-walking is less bouncy. It's a bit like when you're trying to be the first to get to something in school, but Teacher said you're not you're not allowed to run!

Finally, if you like the idea of running but are a bit more of a team player, relays are a great way of working with others. In athletics relays, four people on a team run a certain distance each then pass a baton to the next runner.

Jumping!

There are four main jumping events in athletics: pole vault, high jump, long jump and triple jump.

Pole vaulting involves flinging yourself over a very high bar onto a mat on the other side. You are given a very long stick to help you get up high enough, then you run, launch yourself into the air, go over the bar and fall!

The high jump is where you fling yourself over a not-as-high bar onto a mat on the other side. You are not given anything to help you get up high enough; you just run, jump, get over the bar and land!

A lot of people ask what the difference is between the long jump and the triple jump. In the long jump, you run, take off from a board with one foot and land in a sand pit with your feet together. The triple jump has a hop, a step and finally a jump into the sandpit.

Throwing!

If athletes are not flinging themselves over bars, they might be flinging one of four objects across a field: a shot put, a discus, a javelin or a hammer. A shot put is a metal ball, a discus is like a heavy Frisbee, a javelin is like a spear and a hammer is not like a hammer at all! It is like a shot put on the end of a cord attached to a handle. When you throw the hammer, you spin around before letting it go. Just make sure you don't let go too soon!

Running and jumping!

If you think that you might get bored during a running race, maybe hurdles or steeplechase is the event for you. Hurdles is like horse jumping without the horse. For 100m/110 m/400m hurdle races, you have to jump over ten hurdles. For 60m races, there are only five.

A steeplechase is like an obstacle course where you climb over and leap across obstacles along the way. There is often water involved, so be prepared to get a bit wet!

Running, jumping and throwing!

There are athletes who compete in different events as part of one contest. They earn points in each event and the overall winner is the athlete who scores the most. The main ones are the pentathlon, the heptathlon and the decathlon:

A pentathlon has five events (*penta* means 'five'): fencing, freestyle swimming, equestrian show jumping, pistol shooting and cross country running.

A heptathlon has seven events (*hepta* means 'seven') carried out over two days: three running events, two jumping events and two throwing events.

A decathlon has ten events (*deca* means 'ten'), carried out over two days: four running events, three jumping events and three throwing events.

Did you know?

In the ancient Greek Olympics, the pentathlon included a race from one end of the stadium to the other, a long jump, a discus throw and a javelin throw. The best two competitors in these four events then got to have a wrestling match to decide who was the overall winner!

That's funny!

What word begins and ends with E but only has one letter?
Envelope!

How do you make one disappear?
Add a 'g' and it's gone!

What is as big as a hippo but weighs nothing at all?
A hippo's shadow!

What has a head and a tail but no body?
A coin!

What five-letter word becomes shorter when you add two letters to the end?
Short!

Which knight had a round table?
Sir Cumference!

What kind of haircuts to bees get?
Buzzzzzcuts!

What happens when a ghost gets lost in the fog?
He is mist!

What does a witch use to do her hair?
Scarespray!

62

Why couldn't the pirates play cards?
Because they were standing on the deck!

Did you know all books in the school library are the same colour?
They're all red!

What's the most important thing in your pencil case?
The ruler!

What do you always get on your birthday?
A year older!

Why were the fish's grades bad?
They were below sea level!

What word is always spelled wrong in the dictionary?
Wrong!

Where does stationery go on holiday?
Pencil-vania!

Where do sharks go on holiday?
Finland!

What's green and hangs from the ceiling at Christmas?
A mistle-toad!

What part of the fish weighs the most?
The scales!

What did the bald man say when he got a comb for Christmas?
'I'll never part with it!'

What's missing?

The second picture in each puzzle has one item missing. Circle the missing item.

A

B

Answers on page 80

Cad atá in easnamh?

Tá earra amháin in easnamh sa dara pictiúr de gach puzal. Tarraing ciorcal timpeall an rud atá in easnamh.

C

D

Freagraí ar leathanach 80

65

SORT YOUR STUFF!

What is recycling?
Recycling cleans our waste and turns it into new products or back into the same thing again. This can only happen if we sort our rubbish properly.

Sorting waste just takes a min, Know which bin to put it in!

Why should we recycle?
When a container or packaging is made, a lot of raw materials (the ingredients to make the plastic, cardboard or glass) are used. These ingredients come from our planet.

How can kids help?
Make sure your recycled rubbish is clean. If stuff in our recycle bins has a lot of food dirt on it, the whole lot might have to go to landfill. What a waste!

Rinse plastic, glass and tin containers and let them dry before throwing them in the right bin. **Remember!** Don't run the tap for ages!

Separate the packaging and containers in your recycle bin so they are loose, e.g. don't leave the plastic bag from your cereal in the cardboard box when you put it in the recycling bin.

Did you know…
Plastic bottles can be recycled up to 7 times!
Glass bottles and jars can be recycled forever!

Did you know…
Plastic is made from trees, coal, natural gas, salt and oil.
Glass is made with sand and limestone.
Cardboard/paper is made from trees and plants.

Rinse it, dry it, keep it loose, So it's good for further use!

So you see, recycling makes sense, but it only works if everyone does their bit.

Look for the logo!

This year, we started using the Deposit Return Scheme in Ireland. Most drinks will now have a label with the Re-turn logo. This means that when you buy a drink, you can get back some of the money you pay if you recycle the bottle in the right way.

What containers are not included in the recycling scheme?

Glass bottles and jars, dairy containers (milk, yogurt, butter and cheese) and containers that hold over three litres are not included. Look for the logo!

Get back some money that you pay, Recycle in the Re-turn way!

Where can I return my containers?

You can bring your containers to any shop that sells bottles or cans with the Re-turn logo. You can bring your containers into the shop or ask your mum or dad to show you how the Reverse Vending Machine (RVM) works. The machine reads the barcode on the label after you put it in. Only put in one item at a time.

Do I have to leave the cap on?

You can return your bottles with or without the bottle cap. But if you leave the cap on, the cap will be properly recycled. It also helps the bottle keep its shape and this makes it easier for the machine to read the barcode. New bottles have the caps attached to make this easier.

Follow the recycling trail to find out what your waste can be recycled into if sorted properly.

Who? When? Where?

Who?

1. 2.  3. 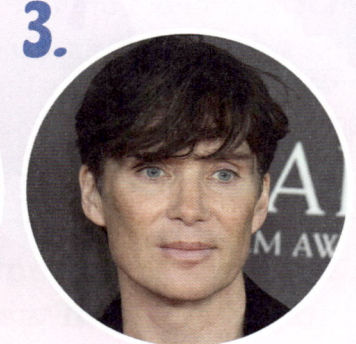 4.

When?

1. 2.

3.  4.

Where?

1. 2.  3.  4.

Check your answers on page 80.

MONSTER Maths

Help Mungo work out each dice sum.

1. 6 − 3 = ☐
2. 3 + 6 = ☐
3. 5 + 4 = ☐
4. 5 − 3 = ☐

5. 5 = ☐ + ☐
6. ☐ = ☐ + ☐
7. ☐ = ☐ + ☐
8. ☐ = ☐ + ☐

9. ☐ + 4 = 6
10. 5 − ☐ = 4
11. 4 + 1 = 9
12. 3 + ☐ = 8

Mango needs to match each shape to its name. He's done one, can you help him do the rest?

Remember, *penta* means five, *hexa* means six, and rectangles can be wide or long!

Sonya Square A.
Reggie Rectangle
Chris Cross
Stevie Star
Paul Parallelogram
Penny Pentagon
Una U
Trina Triangle
Arlo Arrow
Owen O
Orla Octagon
Rowan Rectangle
Cissie Circle
Ollie Oval
Debbie Diamond
Sunny Semi-circle

Answers on page 80

The Friend Books

It was coming up to the Christmas holidays in St Kevin's Boarding School. All the other pupils and most of the staff had gone to the football final away against Cookstown and wouldn't be back for hours. Natalia and Dylan had volunteered to stay behind to keep Flo company. She had recently been in hospital and couldn't travel to the match.

They didn't mind. They loved their school. St Kevin's was the best school in the country! It was a grand old building with creeping ivy, mossy stone statues and a tree-lined drive. They waved the bus off and headed to the library.

The library was big with high ceilings, arched windows and lots of polished wood. Shelves creaked with hundreds of new, old and very old books. It was a dusty room with a musty roof. And that roof was leaking. The pupils had been busy fundraising for a new one: cake sales, jumble sales and sponsored runs, walks and silences. The sponsored silences were held in the library to make it easier to remember to stay quiet! But they had only raised half of what they needed.

The library books were heading into storage and the part of the library containing the oldest books was to be boxed up first. The three pals had been asked to help with the massive task of organising the books into labelled boxes. The children were so excited to help. The teacher in charge of the library was called Ms Blackburn, but the children called her Blackbird because she was always singing. She secretly loved her nickname!

'Oh good morning, children!' announced Ms Blackburn cheerfully. 'Thanks for coming to help. We've so much work to do and, quite frankly,' she said looking up, 'I'm not sure how much time we have.'

The children looked up to the ceiling where a bulging droplet of rainwater was just about to fall into the already quarter-full bucket below.

She went on to explain the importance of packing the books carefully and labelling the boxes clearly. 'Some of these books are very old and we need to keep track of what they are and where they go.'

Some of the books looked ancient and had brown spots on a few of the pages.

'Why do some of the old books have freckles?' asked Natalia.

Ms Blackburn laughed. 'Those brown spots are called foxing,' she explained. 'It's a bit like rust for paper.'

'What's this?' asked Dylan, holding up a small rectangle of card that he had taken out of a little paper pocket on the inside of a book cover.

'It's an old borrowing card. Every library book in the old school system had one. When you borrowed a book, the name of the book and the return date was recorded and filed under your name or library number. The cards were then kept in little wooden drawers like this one,' she said, holding up a little chest of drawers that looked like doll's furniture. 'We've kept all the old records, but I don't think anyone's used them in a long time. With the modern system, we just scan them in and out.'

'Just think, there are books here that have sat on these shelves for decades,' marvelled Flo as she flicked through a dusty copy of *A Christmas Carol* by Charles Dickens. 'I've checked this title out from the school library, but it was a newer version of the book. I wonder if my great-grandparents read this one I'm holding now?'

'Eh, Ms Blackburn, what's that up there?' Natalia asked, pointing to a wooden box on one of the highest shelves.

Ms Blackburn looked up thoughtfully. 'Well, that is a potential solution to some of our money problems. Hang on, I'll show you ...'

She wheeled the library ladder along the rails until it was under the box. After securing the ladder, she carefully climbed a few steps to get it down.

She set the box on the table, wiped the dust off it and put on a pair of white cotton gloves.

'Flo, could you please open the box for me?' she asked.

Flo gently lifted the lid off the box. Ms Blackburn opened back layers of protective paper to reveal a very old and very ornate book. The cover had beautiful artwork embossed in gold.

'It is a first edition of a very famous book by the popular children's author Mo Millington. This was the very first one and it's signed by the author.'

'I've read loads of her books and I've heard of this!' exclaimed Dylan excitedly. 'This is one of the 'friend' books by Mo Millington. Look – there's an inscription inside the cover ...'

Look at my name in order to find
One of a pair, yet one of a kind
Never forget the person behind
To see my friend, have an open MIND.

'Yes, Mo was a pupil at St Kevin's, oh I'd say about 75 years ago,' explained Ms Blackburn. 'She loved this school, especially the library.'

She went on to explain how Mo went on to write fabulous mystery stories, which sold lots of copies all over the world. When Mo was older she visited the school and presented this copy of her last and most famous book to the school library.

'Then,' continued Ms Blackburn, 'just like a plot in one of her mystery stories, she announced that there was a "friend" book, a sequel or "part two" to this one, but we had to work out where it was hidden in the library. Sadly, she died suddenly soon after, having never told anyone where it was. No one has ever found the book. It is a complete conundrum. However, if we ever do find it, we will own the copyright and we can publish copies to sell and we'll get to keep both books.'

'Either way, we have this one and, while it is precious, it can go up for auction next month to help fund repairs to the library. We desperately need the money towards fixing the roof. If the work isn't done soon, we'll lose the whole library, not just a few books.' And with that she moved another bucket to catch a new drip plopping down from the ceiling.

Ms Blackburn folded the paper around the book again and carefully placed it back in the box. She closed the lid and set the box to one side.

'I might as well pack this while we have it down. But first, I'm going to get a cup of tea. I won't be long.'

Ms Blackburn walked towards the door to make the long trek to the staffroom on the other side of the school. She seemed a little sad.

'Poor Blackbird! She loves this school, and she adores her library,' said Natalia.

'I know,' said Flo. 'Let's work extra hard to help her save as many books as possible.'

The children continued their work packing the books for storage in silence, each of them lost in thought.

'I can't get that clue out of my head,' said Flo, finally. 'I've been repeating it over and over again to see if I can make any sense of it.'

'Me too!' said Dylan

'Me three!' announced Natalia. 'I was also wondering if staff members have to use a card to borrow books from the school library or is it just us kids because they don't trust us to bring them back?'

'I don't think it's because they don't trust us, I think they just need to keep track of where the books are,' smiled Flo.

'Ooh, I'd love to know what books Mo Millington took out!' sighed Dylan.

Natalia nudged Flo and nodded over to the little wooden drawers. 'Come on, let's find out!'

'Ok, it looks like they are filed by surname,' said Flo, skimming the cards. Eh, ... K ... L ... M ... Ma ... Me ... Mi ... Mil ... MILL ... Millington, here we go!'

The children peered at the card to see the list of books. *The House of Arden, Anne of Green Gables, Emil and the Detectives* ... the list was really long.

'I haven't heard of most of these, but I think *Anne of Green Gables* is on Netflix now!' laughed Dylan.

'Quick, I think I hear Blackbird coming,' whispered Natalia. 'Put the card back in the filing drawer!'

Flo hurriedly tried to find the place for the card. 'Eh, MICH ... Michaels, no, it's after that. MIND ... Minden no, that's the person behind. Oh wow!'

'Hurry up, Flo!' Dylan whispered loudly.

'Too late!' chuckled Ms Blackburn, walking in clutching her cup.

'We were just interested to see if teachers had to sign books out of the library like us,' explained Dylan.

'And, if so, what books Mo Millington borrowed,' added Natalia.

'That's just a healthy curiosity,' said Ms Blackbird. 'Flo, you look a little pale – is everything ok?'

'Em, a bit better than ok, Blackbird, I mean Ms Blackburn,' said Flo, now blushing.

Natalia and Dylan turned to stare at their friend.

'I think we might have a lead – look!' Flo handed Ms Blackburn the library card she held in her hand.

'But this isn't Millington, it's Minden,' said Ms Blackburn, confused.

'I know but look at the reference letters in the corner "M-I-N-D" and it's the "person behind" Mo's card when you look at her "name in order",' said Flo, quoting bits of the inscription from the book.

Now it was Ms Blackburn's turn to go pale. 'Oh my goodness! Hmm, Alice Minden ... Alice Minden ... Now, why do I recognise that name?' thought Ms Blackburn out loud. 'Oh, I've got it!'

She rushed over to a different section of the library and fished out one of the many Mo Millington children's books from a shelf.

'There!' she pointed at the dedication near the front of the book: '*To Alice Minden, my best reading friend.*'

Natalia took Mo Millington's library card back out of the little drawer. She started comparing the books that Alice had borrowed from the library with the ones on Mo's card. They were exactly the same. Every time Alice borrowed a book, she would return it and then Mo would take it out from the library after her.

'Show me that for a second, please,' said Dylan. 'What was the last book they borrowed ... *The Hundred and One Dalmatians* – let's see if we can find it!'

Ms Blackburn looked up the reference and brought the children to the correct shelf in the old book section. She reached up to get the book and held her breath as she carefully opened it. It fell open at a bookmarked page ...

Ms Blackburn scanned both pages to see if she could spot something, a note scribbled in the margin, anything. But there was nothing. Then, just as she was about to give up, she noticed the bookmark.

'Mo Millington, you little beauty!' exclaimed Ms Blackburn and she held up the bookmark for the children to see. There, in neat handwriting was a set of directions from the spot where they stood to where the book was hidden - behind an old piece of loose wood panelling at the base of a bookshelf ...

******

'Do you know why I think Mo chose that book as our clue?' said Ms Blackburn as she hugged the discovered book. 'The main message in *The Hundred and One Dalmatians* is that sometimes in life you can achieve more as part of a team and when you work together. How right she was.'

They heard the triumphant cheers of the pupils arriving back from Cookstown. The team had managed to save a last-minute goal to win the match. And as Blackbird and her three helpers left the library, they knew that they had managed to save something too.

The End

Dear!

Dear clúdach le haghaidh leabhar le cumhachtaí draíochta.

> Cuir teideal iontach ar do leabhar!

Puzail

Críochnaigh an tsraith le ceann de na freagraí thíos.

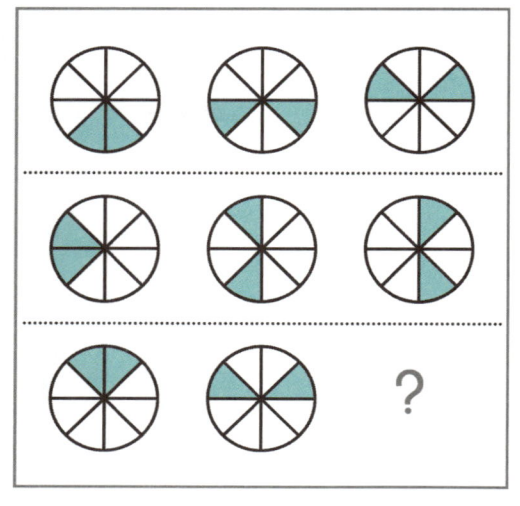

ROGHNAIGH FREAGRA.

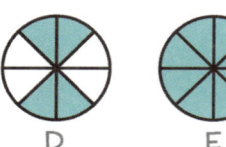

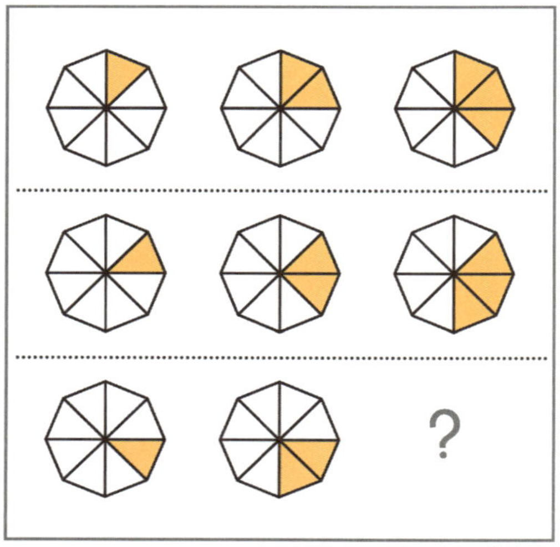

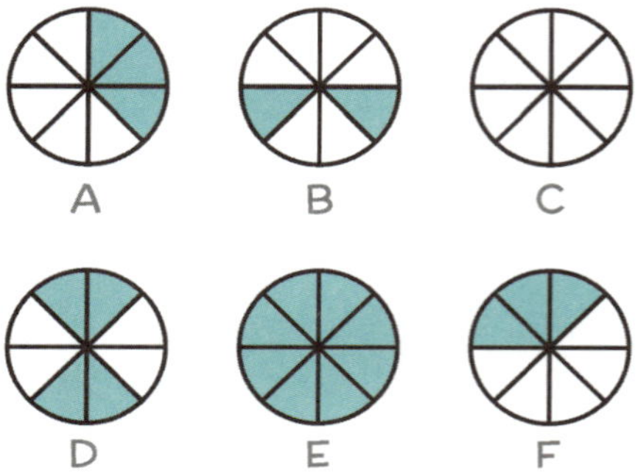

A B C
D E F

ROGHNAIGH FREAGRA.

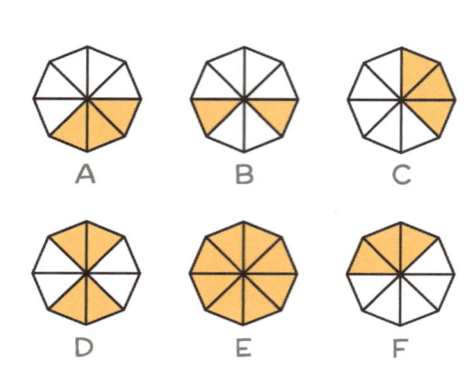

A B C
D E F

Ag féachaint síos!

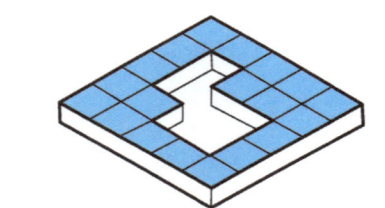

1 Cén chuma atá ar an bpirimid seo ó dhearcadh thuas?

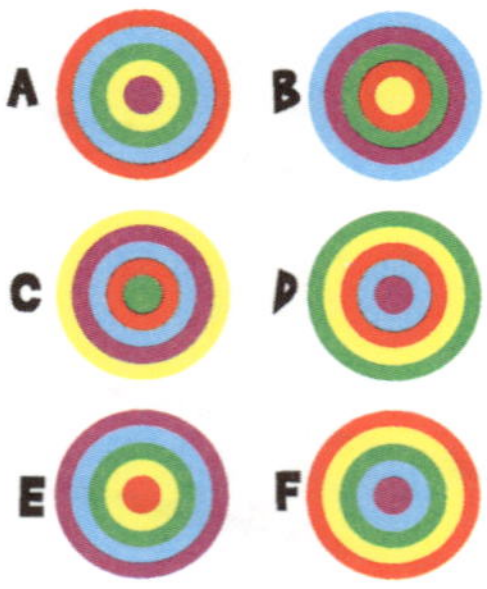

A B
C D
E F

2 Aimsigh an píosa atá in easnamh.

A B
C D
E F

3 Cén chuma atá ar an gciúb seo ó dhearcadh thuas?

A B
C D
E F

Freagraí ar leathanach 80

DRAW!

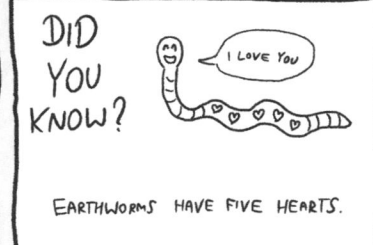

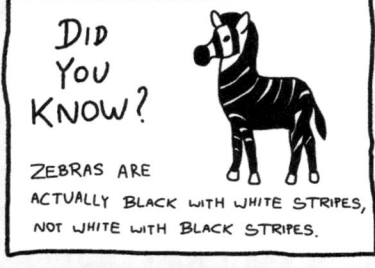

DID YOU KNOW? AN ANT CAN LIFT 50 TIMES ITS OWN WEIGHT.

DID YOU KNOW? EARTHWORMS HAVE FIVE HEARTS.

DID YOU KNOW? HUMAN DNA AND BANANA DNA ARE 50% THE SAME.

DID YOU KNOW? GIRAFFES ONLY SLEEP 30 MINUTES IN A 24-HOUR PERIOD.

DID YOU KNOW? ZEBRAS ARE ACTUALLY BLACK WITH WHITE STRIPES, NOT WHITE WITH BLACK STRIPES.

DID YOU KNOW? A FEMALE RABBIT CAN GIVE BIRTH TO 183 BABIES PER YEAR.

DID YOU KNOW? KOALAS SLEEP 22 HOURS A DAY ON AVERAGE.

DID YOU KNOW? THE YOUNGEST POPE WAS ONLY 11 YEARS OLD.

DID YOU KNOW? THE TALLEST LIVING DOG IS A 1.18 M TALL GREAT DANE.

Have a go at drawing a cartoon for this fact!

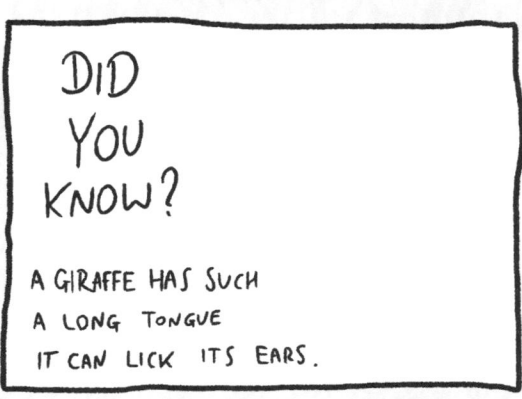

DID YOU KNOW? A GIRAFFE HAS SUCH A LONG TONGUE IT CAN LICK ITS EARS.

Look up a toilet fact to add to this cartoon!

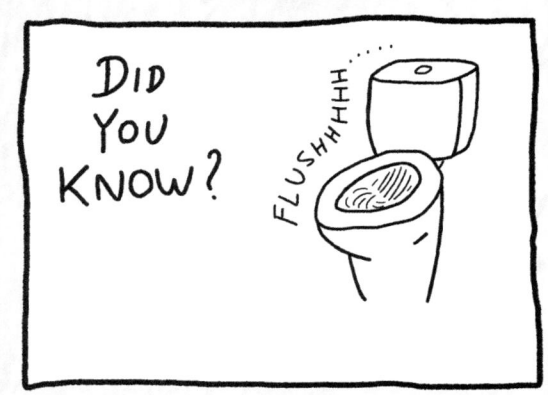

DID YOU KNOW?

Write two other facts you know (or look them up) and draw a cartoon for each.

DID YOU KNOW?

DID YOU KNOW?

75

That's funny!

Knock, knock!
Who's there?
Goat!
Goat who?
Goat the front door and find out!

Knock, knock!
Who's there?
Anita!
Anita who?
Anita use the bathroom, please open the door!

Knock, knock!
Who's there?
Theodore!
Theodore who?
Theodore wasn't open, so I knocked!

Knock, knock!
Who's there?
Wendy!
Wendy who?
Wendy bell gonna be fixed?

Knock, knock!
Who's there?
Luke!
Luke who?
Luke out the window and see!

Knock, knock!
Who's there?
Adam!
Adam who?
Adam my way, I'm coming in!

Knock, knock!
Who's there?
Spell!
Spell who?
W-H-O!

TARRAING

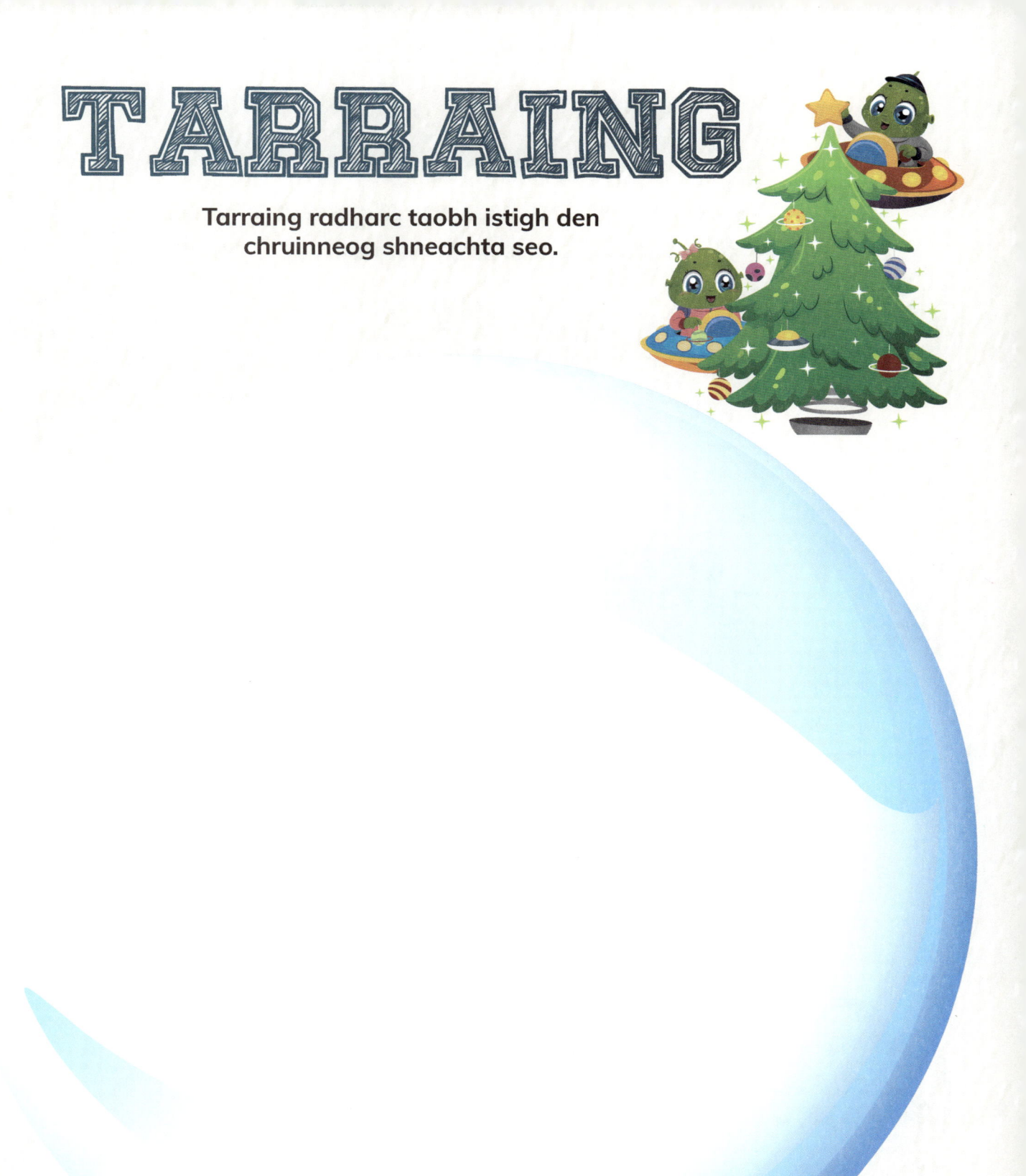

Tarraing radharc taobh istigh den chruinneog shneachta seo.

# Time it!

Race your friends to find these images in your *Parade*.
Write down the page number of each as you find it!

1. P_____
2. P_____
3. P_____
4. P_____
5. P_____
6. P_____
7. P_____
8. P_____
9. P_____
10. P_____
11. P_____
12. P_____
13. P_____
14. P_____
15. P_____
16. P_____
17. P_____
18. P_____
19. P_____
20. P_____

Answers on page 80

78

Answers/Freagraí

Pages 4/5 Get Ready for Christmas!
1. Fairytale of **New** York, 2. All I Want for Christmas is **You**, 3. The **Twelve** Days of Christmas, 4. **Last** Christmas, 5. Santa Claus is Coming to **Town**, 6. **Wonderful** Christmastime, 7. I Wish it Could be Christmas **Every** Day, 8. Merry Christmas **Everyone**, 9. Driving **Home** for Christmas, 10. Rockin' Around the Christmas **Tree**, 11. Let it Snow! Let it Snow! Let it **Snow**! 12. **Frosty** the Snowman, 13. **White** Christmas, 14. It's the Most Wonderful Time of the **Year**, 15. Have Yourself a **Merry** Little Christmas, 16. **Mistletoe** and Wine, 17. I Want a **Hippopotamus** for Christmas, 18. When a **Child** is Born, 19. **Rudolph** the Red-Nosed Reindeer, 20. **Winter** Wonderland, 21. It's Beginning to Look a Lot Like **Christmas**, 22. The Little **Drummer** Boy, 23. We **Wish** You a Merry Christmas, 24. **Jingle** Bells, 25. **Hark** the Herald Angels Sing, 26. **Silent** Night, 27. The **Holly** and the Ivy, 28. Deck the **Halls**, 29. Here Comes Santa **Claus**, 30. Do They Know it's **Christmas**?

Page 14 Science and Nature Quiz
1. 8, 2. Oak, 3. Nostrils, 4. Weather, 5. 3, 6. Bamboo, 7. Eye, 8. 0°C, 9. Skull, 10. A star, 11. An eye doctor, 12. A fish, 13. Lava, 14. Australia, 15. Diamond.

Page 15 Puzail
Ulchabhán

Page 22 Monster Maths
A. 3, 1, 4
B. 2, 1, 3
C. 1, 3, 5
D. 1, 6, 3

Page 23 Tangled!
Bow 1 = blue, Bow 2 = orange, Bow 3 = yellow, Bow 4 = green, Bow 5 = pink. Shadow 7.

Page 24 Sports and Hobbies Quiz
1. 52, 2. Surfing, 3. Fishing rod, 4. Keys, 5. 1, 6. Pirouette, 7. Camogie, hurling and football, 8. 3, 9. Goggles, 10. Knitting, 11. Jigsaw, 12. Rudder, 13. Yellow, 14. Javelin, 15. Plectrum or pick.

Page 25 Crosfhocal

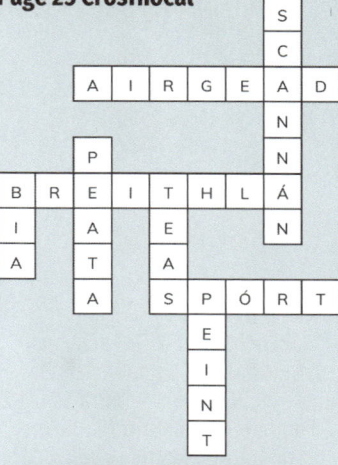

Page 26/27 Look Again!
1. Acorn, 2. Tin top, 3. Chestnut, 4. Xylophone, 5. Scrunched paper, 6. Cotton buds, 7. Matches, 8. Toilet rolls, 9. Shoes/boots, 10. Lipstick, 11. Plug hole, 12. Fairy lights, 13. Laptop, 14. Telescope, 15. Hat, 16. Merry-go-round horse, 17. Ladle, 18. Measuring tape, 19. Slinky, 20. Keys, 21. Sticky tape, 22. Tree, 23. Skateboard, 24. Screwdriver, 25. Log pile.

Page 29
chocolate coins, lollipops, sweets, bubble gum, mini chocolate bars

Page 31 Puzail
Crúiscín: F, Cupán: O, Pota plandaí: A

Page 32/33 Aimsigh na Difríochtaí

Page 34 How many?/Cé mhéad?
Pigs: Left 13   Right 15
Sliotanna (sloths): Ar dheis 9   Ar chlé 14

Page 35 Winter Quiz
1. November, December and January, 2. Snowboarding, 3. Mittens, 4. A scarf, 5. Robin, 6. Hot chocolate, 7. Frost, 8. January 6th, 9. Hibernation, 10. Carrot, 11. Evergreen, 12. Salt, 13. January, 14. December 24th, 15. Advent calendar.

Page 40/41 Puzail
15 glais, scáth a naoi

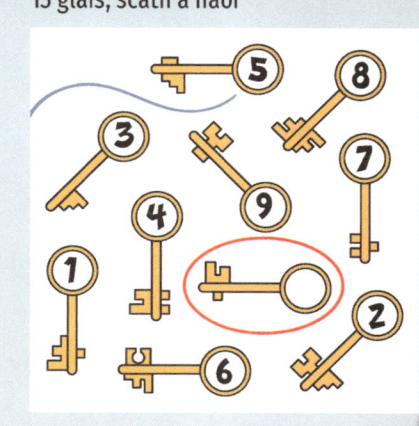

79

1 + 6 = 7, 7 − 2 = 5, 3 + 5 = 8, 6 + 3 = 9, 8 − 6 = 2, 6 − 3 = 3.

Page 42/43 Féach Arís!
1. Arán, 2. Milseáin, 3. Brioscaí, 4. Sú talún, 5. Cnónna, 6. Trátaí stánaithe, 7. Preatsal, 8. Puimcín, 9. Naitseó, 10. Criospa, 11. Uisce, 12. Píotsa, 13. Cáis, 14. Grán rósta, 15. Núdail, 16. Blaosc uibhe, 17. Sceallóga, 18. Cón, 19. Canna, 20. Caife, 21. Bananaí, 22. Anann, 23. Cipíní aráin, 24. Pancóga, 25. Pasta. Téama: Bia

Page 46/47 Puzzles

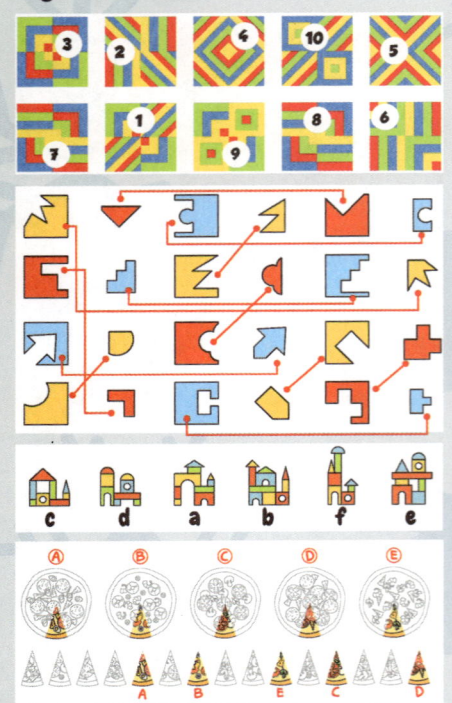

Page 51 Snow Business

Page 54/55 Souped up!
Aubergine

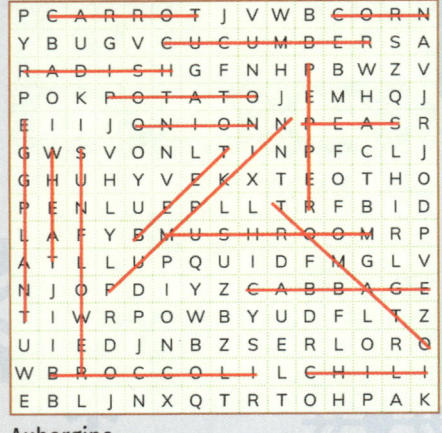

Page 56 General Knowledge Quiz
1. The rook, 2. Dance, 3. Canada, 4. Tigger, 5. Budapest, 6. Neptune, 7. Two. (A squid has ten arms. Two of their arms are longer than the other eight and are called tentacles), 8. Jack Black 9. Eggplant, 10. Neptune, 11. Barbie, 12. Molars, 13. Pink, 14. Dua Lipa, 15. Index.

Page 57 Tangled!
A5, B1, C3, D4, E7, F2, G6.
Shadow 9.

Page 58/59 Féach Arís!
1. Stáplóir, 2. Crochadán, 3. Spéaclaí, 4. Cuachóg, 5. Buidéal, 6. Cás spéaclaí, 7. Fáiscín páipéir, 8. Bréagán, 9. Dúradán, 10. Gobán, 11. Feadáin cairtchláir, 12. Barbie, 13. Srónbheannach, 14. Lacha rubair, 15. Crú capaill, 16. Peann aibhsithe, 17. Uaireadóir, 18. Liathróid chispheile, 19. Peann luaidhe, 20. Fón, 21. Teidí, 22. Bó, 23. Friochtán, 24. Bolgáin, 25. Toirtís.

Page 64/65 What's Missing?

Page 68 Who? When? Where? Quiz
Who?
1. Katie McCabe
2. Taylor Swift
3. Cillian Murphy
4. Patrick Kielty

When?
1. St Patrick's Day, March 17
2. Valentine's Day, February 14
3. Halloween, October 31
4. Christmas Day, December 25

Where?
1. Dublin, 2. Paris, 3. London, 4. New York

Page 69 Monster Maths

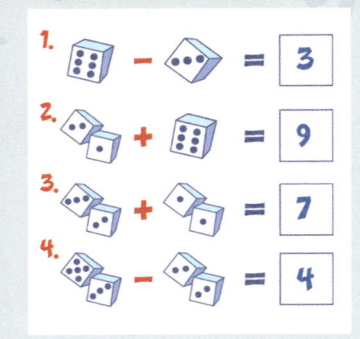

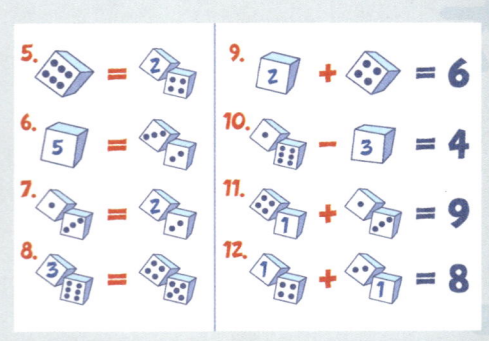

A. Sonya Square, B. Reggie Rectangle, C. Paul Parallelogram, D. Orla Octagon, E. Rowan Rectangle, F. Una U, G. Trina Triangle, H. Cissie Circle, I. Debbie Diamond, J. Chris Cross, K. Stevie Star, L. Ollie Oval, M. Sunny Semi-circle, N. Arlo Arrow, O. Owen O, P. Penny Pentagon.

Page 74 Puzail
B, A. Ag féachaint síos: F, E, B

Page 78 Time it!
1. P 69, 2. P 68, 3. P 37, 4. P 4, 5. P 7, 6. P 66, 7. P 63, 8. P 22, 9. P 57, 10. P 69, 11. P 38, 12. P 14, 13. P 62, 14. P 17, 15. P 50, 16. P 12, 17. P 24, 18. P 30, 19. P 35, 20. P 56.